OCCASIONAL PAPER 100

The Gambia:
Economic Adjustment
in a Small Open Economy

Michael T. Hadjimichael, Thomas Rumbaugh, and Eric Verreydt,
with Philippe Beaugrand and Christopher Chirwa

INTERNATIONAL MONETARY FUND
Washington DC
October 1992

© 1992 International Monetary Fund

Cataloging-in-Publication Data

Hadjimichael, Michael T.
  The Gambia : economic adjustment in a small open economy /
Michael T. Hadjimichael, Thomas Rumbaugh and Eric Verreydt with
Philippe Beaugrand and Christopher Chirwa. — Washington, DC :
International Monetary Fund, 1992.
    p. cm. — (Occasional paper, 0251-6365 ; 100)
  Includes bibliographical references.
  ISBN 1-55775-230-3
  1. Structural adjustment (Economic policy) — Gambia. I. Rumbaugh,
Thomas. II. Verreydt, Eric. III. Title. IV. Series : Occasional paper
(International Monetary Fund) ; no. 100.
HC1070 .H23 1992

Price: US$15.00
(US$12.00 to full-time faculty members and
students at universities and colleges)

Please send orders to:
International Monetary Fund, Publication Services
700 19th Street, N.W., Washington, D.C. 20431, U.S.A.
Tel.: (202) 623-7430   Telefax: (202) 623-7201

Contents

Tables

Section

Charts

Section

The following symbols have been used throughout this paper:

. . . to indicate that data are not available;

— to indicate that the figure is zero or less than half the final digit shown, or that the item does not exist;

– between years or months (e.g., 1991–92 or January–June) to indicate the years or months covered, including the beginning and ending years or months;

/ between years (e.g., 1991/92) to indicate a crop or fiscal (financial) year.

"Billion" means a thousand million.

Minor discrepancies between constituent figures and totals are due to rounding.

The term "country," as used in this paper, does not in all cases refer to a territorial entity that is a state as understood by international law and practice; the term also covers some territorial entities that arc not states, but for which statistical data are maintained and provided internationally on a separate and independent basis.

Preface

This paper is based on the staff report and the background paper prepared in connection with the consultations between the Fund and The Gambia in 1992 and includes information available through May 1992. The authors are indebted to Anupam Basu, Christian Brachet, Evangelos Calamitsis, Jean Clément, Christian François, and Susan Schadler for their valuable comments and suggestions. They also would like to thank Janet Bungay for editorial advice, Yvette Conell and Abdul Mahar for secretarial assistance, and Juanita Roushdy of the External Relations Department for editing and coordinating the paper for publication. The authors bear sole responsibility for any factual errors.

The opinions expressed in the paper are those of the authors and should not be construed as those of the Government of The Gambia, Executive Directors of the IMF, or other members of the IMF staff.

I Introduction

The Gambia is a very small country located on the west coast of Africa, surrounded on three sides by Senegal, extending inland at widths varying from 24 to 48 kilometers along the banks of the River Gambia, with a total area of 10,700 square kilometers. With a population of about 890,000, which is rising at a rate of 3.4 percent a year, The Gambia has one of the highest population densities in the world (estimated at 207 inhabitants per square kilometer of agricultural land in 1991). It has also a fairly undeveloped human capital base, with an illiteracy rate of 75 percent and a primary school enrollment rate of 56 percent (in 1987).

The Gambia has an open economy with limited natural resources and is one of the least developed African countries, with a per capita income estimated at present at $325. The traditional mainstay of economic activity has been the production and export of groundnuts, although in recent years significant progress has been made in diversifying production and exports toward tourism and trade services. Most of the population work in agriculture, which accounts for about 20 percent of real GDP; industry contributes 12 percent of value added, with the rest accounted for by services.

The Gambia became independent in 1965 and since then has been governed by a democratic multiparty parliamentary system, with free elections held at regular intervals.[1]

During the first ten years after independence, broadly stable macroeconomic conditions were maintained with modest rates of economic growth. In the decade to 1985/86, however, external shocks and inappropriate domestic policies caused economic and financial performance to deteriorate markedly. In particular, unfavorable weather, erratic world groundnut prices, and inadequate real producer prices led to a sharp decline in the domestic output of groundnuts. During the same period, the involvement of the public sector in the economy increased sharply, through the creation of several public enterprises, particularly in the industrial

and trading sectors, and the size of the Central Government rose markedly, entailing, inter alia, a doubling of the size of the civil service. The resulting large expansion in government current expenditure, coupled with a surge in government development expenditure, contributed to a widening of fiscal imbalances. The expansionary stance of fiscal policy and an increasingly overvalued currency boosted the demand for imports and discouraged the surrender of export proceeds to the official banking system, inducing a growing external indebtedness and a depletion of gross official reserves. As a consequence, the growth of output in the directly productive sectors of the economy (i.e., excluding government services) remained low, inflation accelerated, and major external disequilibria emerged. Although the pressures on the external current account position were alleviated somewhat by large inflows of external assistance and some partial adjustment measures in the early 1980s, the imbalances reached critical proportions by the end of 1985/86. Gross official reserves fell to the equivalent of less than a week of imports, external public debt climbed to 113 percent of GDP, and external payments arrears peaked at SDR 88.2 million (almost one and one half times the 1985/86 export earnings, including net re-exports and travel income), of which SDR 10.3 million represented overdue obligations to the Fund.

In response to the rapidly deteriorating situation, the Gambian authorities in June 1985 began to implement a comprehensive adjustment program, the Economic Recovery Program (ERP), aimed at restoring financial equilibrium and laying the foundation for sustainable economic growth. In 1990, the ERP was succeeded by the Program for Sustained Development (PSD), which continued the thrust of ERP policies, while renewing efforts to stimulate private sector development. The Gambia's adjustment efforts have been supported by successive arrangements from the Fund, comprising two annual arrangements under the structural adjustment facility (SAF) during 1986/87–1987/88 (July/June) and a three-year arrangement under the enhanced structural adjustment facility (ESAF)

---

[1] For an overview of recent political developments, see Sallah (1990).

during 1988/89–1990/91, as well as a stand-by arrangement and a drawing under the compensatory financing facility during 1986/87. The total cumulative use of Fund resources by The Gambia amounted to the equivalent of SDR 38.91 million, or 227.5 percent of quota. Substantial financial and technical assistance has also been provided by the World Bank, including two structural adjustment credits, and by other bilateral and multilateral donors.

With successful implementation of a broad range of financial and structural reforms, The Gambia's economic and financial performance has improved considerably since 1985/86. The Gambia's experience is a good example of economic adjustment, even though it is recognized that more remains to be done, as a number of major structural and institutional constraints continue to hamper the economy. Following the expiration of the three-year ESAF arrangement in November 1991, the Gambian authorities requested a continuation of the close policy dialogue with the Fund and monitoring by the Fund of The Gambia's economic and financial policies for 1992/93, as well as the updating of the policy framework paper to cover the period 1992/93–1994/95.

II Overview of Recent Economic Performance

The economic strategy since 1985/86 has been aimed primarily at substantially reducing the involvement of the public sector in the economy, encouraging the development of the private sector, lowering domestic and external imbalances, and fostering economic growth. Accordingly, the strategy has entailed mainly (1) the early restoration of an appropriate structure of relative prices and a strengthening of economic incentives in the context of a market-oriented approach; (2) the implementation of restrictive fiscal and monetary policies; and (3) the introduction of complementary structural reforms, particularly in the public enterprise and financial sectors.

Adjustment Policies

A notable feature of the adjustment efforts has been the emphasis on strengthening the supply response of the economy and enhancing the efficiency of resource allocation by removing price distortions and government controls, introducing a market-determined exchange rate, and liberalizing the marketing arrangements for groundnuts.

To encourage a return of the foreign exchange proceeds to the official banking system, as well as to stimulate the production of exportables, a flexible exchange rate system was introduced in January 1986 in the context of an interbank market, replacing the peg of the dalasi (the national currency) to the pound sterling. To deepen the foreign exchange market, the enforcement of the Exchange Control Act was suspended at the same time, resulting in a de facto lifting of the exchange restrictions on current and capital international transactions, and licensed foreign exchange bureaus were established in April 1990. The only remaining exchange restriction related to the existence of external payments arrears, which were gradually eliminated in the period to July 1990. Overall, the interbank foreign exchange market has functioned smoothly, resulting in an effective absorption of the parallel foreign exchange market and the virtual elimination of the spread between the exchange rates prevailing in the two markets. Under the new exchange rate regime, the dalasi depreciated by 57 percent in nominal effective terms during 1986, but appreciated gradually by some 18 percent by early 1990 (Chart 1); since then, it has remained broadly stable, fluctuating within a narrow range. The nominal exchange rate adjustments, combined with tight financial policies and progress in lowering inflation has improved The Gambia's external competitiveness markedly. In real effective terms, the dalasi depreciated by 44 percent during 1986, and even though it appreciated somewhat in the period to mid-1989, it has since gradually fallen back to its level at the end of 1986.[2]

The depreciation of the dalasi facilitated marked increases in real producer prices for groundnuts and other cash crops in 1985/86. In fact, to induce a reversal of cross-border sales of groundnuts to a neighboring country, where producer prices have been kept high through government subsidies, producer prices in The Gambia were initially set higher than export prices, necessitating sizable budgetary support to the Gambia Produce Marketing Board (GPMB) to cover operating costs. Groundnut producer prices were lowered in subsequent years to eliminate the need for government subsidies, as well as to reflect the weakening in world groundnut oil prices. In order to liberalize the marketing arrangements for groundnuts, the system of guaranteed producer prices for groundnuts was abolished with effect from the 1989/90 crop year and replaced with new arrangements under which the GPMB announces a

---

[2]Based on the IMF's Information Notice System, under which the effective exchange rate index is calculated as the ratio of the dalasi to a trade-weighted basket of the currencies of 20 industrial and developing trading partner countries, expressed in a common currency. An alternative effective exchange rate index, calculated with updated weights based on trade statistics for 1988–90, covering a subset of trading partners (excluding, notably, Brazil and Argentina), suggests a slightly more depreciating trend for the dalasi since 1989 (see Chart 1).

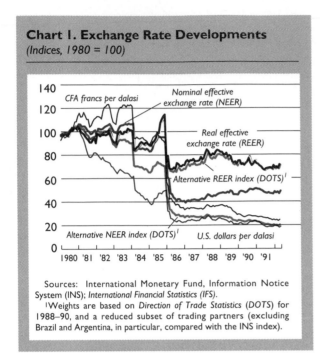

Chart I. Exchange Rate Developments
(Indices, 1980 = 100)

Sources: International Monetary Fund, Information Notice System (INS); *International Financial Statistics (IFS)*.
[1]Weights are based on *Direction of Trade Statistics (DOTS)* for 1988–90, and a reduced subset of trading partners (excluding Brazil and Argentina, in particular, compared with the INS index).

groundnut purchase price at the beginning of the crop year, based on commercial criteria and without any government involvement. In addition, the export monopoly of the GPMB was lifted in October 1990. The subsidies on fertilizers and other agricultural inputs were also eliminated, and the marketing of these inputs liberalized in the early stages of the reform efforts. In addition, all other price controls were lifted, while public utility tariffs and retail prices for petroleum products have been adjusted frequently to reflect changes in the underlying cost structures.

An integral part of the adjustment efforts since 1985/86 has been the pursuit of a restrictive fiscal policy, aimed at lowering the budget deficit (excluding grants) and raising government savings, as well as fostering economic activity. On the revenue side, policies have focused on broadening the tax base, strengthening tax administration, and rationalizing the structure of taxation. Tax reforms have been directed at improving economic incentives and enhancing efficiency and equity in the economy. The reforms included the introduction of a sales tax, reductions in the marginal rates of personal income taxation, abolition of the taxes on exports, and reductions in import tariffs so as to move toward a low and uniform rate of protection, while preserving the tariff incentives for the re-export trade. On the expenditure side, policies

have sought to increase the efficiency of public investment by focusing on the rehabilitation of the basic economic and social infrastructure, while also reorienting current expenditure to facilitate higher provisions for operations and maintenance and social services. In the latter regard, special emphasis has been placed on raising the share in total current spending of outlays on education and health, given the importance attached under the program to improving the country's human capital and paving the way for long-term growth. To facilitate such a restructuring of government spending, the growth of the civil service wage bill has been kept modest.

Overall, the budget deficit (excluding grants) was reduced from a peak of 17 percent of GDP in 1987/88 to an estimated 4 percent in 1991/92. This was achieved despite a boost in government expenditure caused by special budgetary provisions for the repayment of public enterprise debts to the domestic banking system and the takeover by the Government of nonperforming bank loans. The improvement in the fiscal position, together with the available net inflows of external assistance, has allowed the Government to make sizable net repayments to the banking system, thereby accommodating the legitimate financing needs of the private sector and supporting the anti-inflationary stance of monetary policy. The latter has been primarily directed at lowering inflation to a low level comparable to that of trading partner countries, while also achieving the targeted improvement in the overall balance of payments position and the associated buildup of gross official reserves, in a framework consistent with the targeted expansion in output. To this end, a broadly restrictive monetary and credit policy has been pursued. At the same time, the effectiveness of financial intermediation was enhanced through the lifting of interest rate controls in September 1985, the introduction of an auction system for issuing treasury bills in July 1986, and, more important, a shift to an indirect system of monetary control in September 1990. Since 1986/87, interest rates have been maintained through open market operations at positive levels in real terms (measured in relation to inflation during the previous 12 months) and with appropriate differentials vis-à-vis interest rates abroad, thereby encouraging financial savings and supporting the exchange rate policy.

External policies, for their part, have been aimed at broadening the export base and at containing the debt-service burden by maintaining a liberal exchange and trade system, preserving external competitiveness, and pursuing a prudent external debt-management policy. As indicated above, with the emphasis of financial policies on bringing inflation under control, the nominal effective exchange rate has been kept reasonably stable, after an initial marked decline, in the context of a flexible exchange rate regime, despite occasional fluctuations. This flexibility has cushioned the impact on the economy of the deterioration in The Gambia's external terms of trade (excluding re-exports) and has helped preserve the gains in competitiveness. In its foreign borrowing policy, the Government has relied exclusively on official grants and concessional long-term loans, avoiding any recourse to, or guaranteeing of, external loans on commercial terms; short-term foreign borrowing has also been limited to normal import-financing purposes.

These policies have been complemented by a broad range of structural reforms designed to enhance the efficiency of the economy and stimulate private sector activity. Under the public enterprise reform program, public sector activities that could be more efficiently carried out by the private sector have been scaled back markedly, through the divestiture of some 20 enterprises (almost 60 percent of the total number of public enterprises). In addition, several measures have been taken to improve the financial position of the enterprises remaining in the Government's portfolio, including the signing of performance agreements. In the financial sector, the reform efforts have focused on improving the efficiency of the intermediation process and encompassed the takeover by the Government of nonperforming bank loans, measures to strengthen bank supervision, and the restructuring of the largest commercial bank (The Gambia Commercial and Development Bank (GCDB)), which was owned by the Government, culminating in its privatization in June 1992. Furthermore, a tourism development area has been designated and a new Investment Code was enacted in 1988, providing a range of fiscal incentives to private investment in export-oriented and import-substituting activities.

Sectoral strategies have been aimed at stimulating the supply response of the economy and exploiting the development potential that exists in the agricultural sector, small-scale manufacturing, fisheries, tourism, entrepôt trade, and other services, supported by the World Bank and other bilateral and multilateral donors. Given the importance of agriculture for the well-being of most of the population, special emphasis has been placed on developing this sector. In particular, policies have been directed at enhancing efficiency in groundnut production, processing, and marketing, as well as diversifying into other cash crops and horticulture, and continued expansion of food crops; these objectives were to be attained through improved applied research and extension services,

and an expanded role of the private sector in output marketing and input supply. Sectoral policies have also focused on improving basic health and education services, reducing the high rate of population growth, and protecting the environment.

The Gambia's economic strategy has been supported by considerable technical and financial assistance from the international donor community. The provision of such assistance, particularly of concessional long-term project and program loans, has responded quickly to the introduction of comprehensive adjustment measures by the Gambian authorities. Total aid disbursements rose from SDR 38 million (19 percent of GDP) in 1985/86 to an annual average of SDR 52 million (25 percent of GDP) in the subsequent five years (Table 1).

Policy Implementation

Policy implementation has been guided by a set of quarterly financial benchmarks and performance criteria, relating to the net domestic assets of the banking system (the Central Bank since September 1990), net credit to the Government by the banking system, gross credit to the GPMB, gross official reserves, the contracting or guaranteeing of new foreign loans by the Government, and the outstanding stock of external payments arrears; quantitative benchmarks on current government expenditure (excluding debt-service payments and contributions to the development fund) have also been set for the last four fiscal years. In addition, several structural benchmarks and structural performance criteria have been set, relating mainly to the divestiture of public enterprises. Overall, policy implementation has been broadly satisfactory. Occasional financial slippages and delays in the implementation of certain structural reforms have caused the nonobservance of a few quantitative and structural benchmarks, but the nonobservance of these benchmarks has resulted mainly from exogenous factors, shortfalls or delays in external assistance, and slippages in the implementation of fiscal and monetary policies induced by special factors or, in a couple of cases, pressures on government expenditure. On some occasions, there have been delays in sterilizing the impact on money supply of higher-than-expected inflows of foreign exchange earnings from tourism and re-exports. In all cases of deviations from the programmed path, the authorities have been quick to adopt corrective measures to help bring the program back on track, usually after consultations with the Fund.

The program for 1986/87–1988/89, supported by two annual arrangements under the SAF and the first annual arrangement under the ESAF, were

Table 1. External Assistance[1]

	1982/83	1983/84	1984/85	1985/86	1986/87	1987/88	1988/89	1989/90	1990/91	1991/92 Est.
					(In millions of SDRs)					
Grants	23.8	23.7	28.6	31.0	32.4	36.2	31.8	34.3	31.9	34.9
Loans	17.1	15.1	12.2	6.6	37.1	14.3	10.0	20.1	13.9	19.4
Project loans	17.1	15.1	12.2	6.6	12.1	12.6	10.0	10.9	9.5	10.1
Program loans	—	—	—	—	25.0	1.7	—	9.2	4.4	9.4
Total	40.9	38.8	40.8	37.6	69.5	50.5	41.8	54.4	45.8	54.3
					(In percent of GDP)					
Grants	10.5	11.9	14.9	15.8	19.8	20.0	15.0	15.4	13.1	14.2
Loans	7.6	7.6	6.3	3.4	22.6	7.9	4.7	9.0	5.7	7.9
Project loans	7.6	7.6	6.3	3.4	7.4	7.0	4.7	4.9	3.9	4.1
Program loans	—	—	—	—	15.2	0.9	—	4.1	1.8	3.8
Total	18.1	19.4	21.2	19.2	42.4	27.9	19.8	24.4	18.8	22.1

Sources: Data provided by the Gambian authorities; and IMF staff estimates.
[1] Including commodity aid and technical assistance.

implemented broadly on schedule. Economic performance weakened somewhat during the first half of 1989/90, the program for which was supported by the second annual ESAF arrangement. A disruption of the re-export trade, due to regional political disturbances, a decline in tourist arrivals, and a shortfall in nonproject grant receipts, curtailed the supply of foreign exchange to the interbank foreign exchange market and exerted downward pressure on the exchange rate of the dalasi. As a result, the quantitative targets for gross official reserves were not observed and the monetary program was shifted off track. With a tightening of fiscal policy during the second half of 1989/90, together with a depreciation of the dalasi earlier in the fiscal year, and a recovery in tourist arrivals and re-exports, the momentum of adjustment was regained.

The program for 1990/91, supported by the third annual ESAF arrangement, was on track for most of the fiscal year. The quantitative benchmarks and performance criteria for the first three quarters were met. However, delays in implementing some envisaged structural reforms caused a postponement of the disbursement of the second tranche of SAC II from the World Bank, including the associated cofinancing. Among the delayed reforms were the strengthening of the management of the GPMB and of customs administration and the completion of public expenditure plans for the priority sectors of the economy. The resulting major shortfall in external assistance, combined with an overrun in government current spending, led to the nonobservance of several of the quantitative benchmarks for the end of June 1991.

The impact of these developments on economic performance was aggravated during the first half of 1991/92: additional shortfalls in external assistance, unrelated to policy implementation, and sizable overruns in government expenditure induced a worrisome acceleration in monetary expansion. As a consequence, several of the indicative quantitative benchmarks for the period were not met. In response, the authorities introduced a package of corrective measures in March 1992, with special emphasis on tax reforms and other measures to strengthen the fiscal stance, designed to bring the program back on track.

Developments Since 1985/86

The implementation of the authorities' economic strategy has resulted in an impressive improvement in The Gambia's economic and financial performance, thus laying the foundation for a sustainable expansion in output. During the six-year period to 1991/92, a steady growth in real GDP was recorded, inflation declined, and the overall balance of payments balance switched from deficits to sizable surpluses, facilitating the gradual elimination of all outstanding external payments arrears and the buildup of a comfortable level of gross official reserves. The external objectives and, to a lesser extent, the inflation targets of the programs supported by the SAF/ESAF arrangements were met, but actual real GDP growth fell somewhat short of the program targets, particularly during the last two fiscal years, owing largely to exogenous factors.

In particular, despite unfavorable weather, which led to a stagnation of agricultural output, real GDP grew on average by 3.4 percent a year, in line with the rapid growth of the population (Chart 2 and Table 2).[3] The vagaries of the weather, together with the downward trend in world groundnut prices, led to sharp fluctuations from year to year in groundnut production. Excluding agriculture, real GDP grew on average by 4.4 percent a year, as activity in the industrial and services sectors expanded strongly, particularly in the dynamic tourism and trade sectors, including the re-export trade. End-of-period inflation, as measured by changes in the consumer price index, declined from 70 percent in 1985/86 to 5 percent in 1990/91, before rising again to 12 percent in 1991/92; in annual average terms, the inflation rate has been more stable, falling from a peak of 46 percent in 1986/87, reflecting largely the impact effect of the exchange rate adjustment, to a range of 9–11 percent in the subsequent five years.

The Gambia's external position has improved substantially since 1985/86. The gains in competitiveness and the enhanced price incentives have encouraged a diversification of the production and export bases, which has more than offset the adverse impact on total foreign exchange proceeds of the virtual stagnation in groundnut export receipts. The increased availability of foreign exchange has facilitated a strong expansion in domestic imports, reflecting to a large extent the increasing project-related imports financed by donors under the public investment program. Overall, the external current account deficit, excluding official transfers, has been contained at about SDR 30–35 million throughout the period since 1985/86, implying a reduction in relation to GDP from a peak of 22 percent in 1986/87 to an estimated 14 percent in 1991/92 (Chart 3 and

Chart 2. Developments in Output and Prices
(Annual percentage changes)

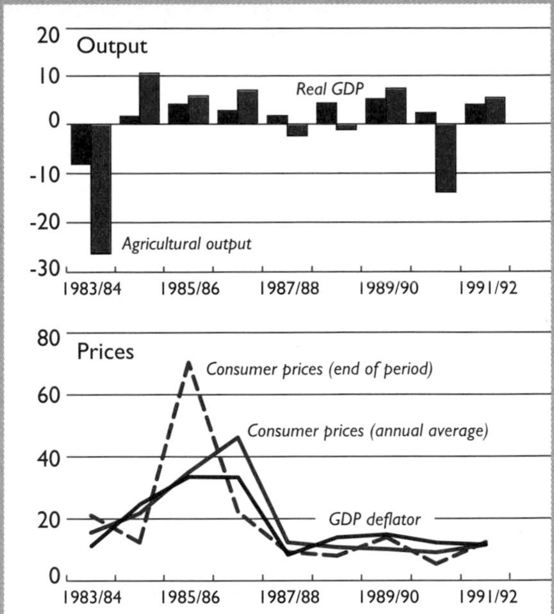

Sources: Data provided by the Gambian authorities; and IMF staff estimates.

Table 3). This deficit has, on average, been covered fully by the inflows of official transfers, while the net disbursements of concessional official loans and the increasing inflows of private investment—reflecting in large part direct investment in the tourism and horticultural sectors—have allowed sizable overall balance of payments surpluses to be recorded in every fiscal year since 1985/86. These surpluses, together with the exceptional financing available from the Fund, as well as debt reschedulings and debt relief,[4] have facilitated a gradual repayment of all outstanding external payments arrears and a strong buildup of gross official reserves. The latter rose from a mere SDR 1.4 mil-

---

[3]Based on revised GDP data. In December 1991, revised national accounts statistics were released by the Central Statistics Department, indicating changes in the composition and the level of real GDP, as well as a significant upward adjustment in the GDP deflator; thus, by 1990/91 nominal GDP was 34 percent higher than previously estimated.

---

[4]Outstanding arrears and debt-service obligations amounting to SDR 17.0 million were rescheduled by Paris Club creditors in September 1986, while arrears and debt of SDR 14.3 million were rescheduled by London Club creditors in January 1988. Debt relief of about SDR 21.9 million, in the form of cancellation of debt-service payments on bilateral loans falling due during 1989–98, was also granted by France in 1989.

Table 2. Selected Economic and Financial Indicators

	1982/83	1983/84	1984/85	1985/86	1986/87	1987/88	1988/89	1989/90	1990/91	1991/92 Est.
	(Annual percentage changes, unless otherwise specified)									
National income and prices[1]										
GDP at constant prices	14.6	−8.2	1.6	4.1	2.8	1.7	4.3	5.2	2.3	4.0
GDP deflator	1.7	10.4	22.1	35.6	33.2	8.2	13.8	14.8	12.1	11.4
Nominal GDP *(in millions of dalasis)*	605.8	617.8	781.9	1,085.2	1,486.0	1,635.5	1,942.3	2,345.2	2,689.4	3,117.2
Consumer price index *(period average)*	9.3	15.6	21.8	35.0	46.2	12.4	10.8	10.2	9.1	11.5
Consumer price index *(end of period)*	11.5	21.1	12.4	70.4	22.3	9.2	8.0	14.0	5.4	12.4
External sector										
Exports, f.o.b. *(in SDRs)*[2]	15.1	11.1	−27.9	−4.6	−5.6	6.1	30.1	20.2	10.3	5.1
Imports, f.o.b. *(in SDRs)*[2]	−4.7	17.6	−22.1	−1.6	6.6	1.7	23.2	24.8	11.2	5.0
Terms of trade[2]	4.9	62.0	−14.2	−41.4	−0.5	−1.5	0.1	−5.5	2.7	−0.2
Nominal effective exchange rate[3]	2.0	−3.7	−13.0	−15.7	−43.6	4.9	8.2	2.1	4.6	−4.7
Real effective exchange rate[3]	1.2	−0.5	−5.2	−1.2	−18.5	7.4	4.2	−8.9	−3.3	−3.6
Government budget										
Revenue and grants	−17.4	25.4	17.7	50.3	78.3	1.1	15.3	16.7	2.9	26.8
Total expenditure and net lending	−3.2	17.8	24.4	9.8	90.0	10.1	−16.2	38.8	−8.0	19.6
Current expenditure	−3.1	24.9	7.7	22.4	76.5	34.4	−19.3	22.4	4.1	10.6
Development expenditure	−3.3	5.7	55.2	−16.5	68.2	14.9	−19.8	22.6	14.6	8.9
Money and credit										
Net domestic assets[4]	89.3	34.6	10.3	121.1	−131.8	−21.2	−8.4	−18.6	−35.9	−52.8
Credit to the Government[4]	24.1	2.9	10.6	4.5	−72.6	8.4	−19.7	−0.0	−32.8	−60.4
Credit to the private sector[4]	19.2	−8.2	0.4	13.5	−4.1	5.5	8.2	6.1	7.9	7.9
Broad money	35.1	3.2	32.9	24.5	43.9	20.5	8.3	17.0	16.9	4.7
Velocity *(GDP/average broad money)*	4.6	4.5	4.3	4.9	5.3	4.5	4.8	4.9	5.1	5.0
Interest rate on treasury bills[5] *(in percent; end of period)*	7.5	9.5	9.5	15.0	19.0	16.8	18.0	17.5	18.5	18.5
	(In percent of GDP)									
Investment and savings										
Gross investment	22.3	22.7	21.2	15.4	19.6	15.5	17.6	20.6	19.3	19.0
Gross national savings	20.8	16.3	17.9	14.7	17.5	19.5	19.4	17.9	19.2	19.3
Of which: domestically generated[6]	(10.3)	(4.4)	(3.0)	(−1.1)	(−2.3)	(−0.5)	(4.4)	(2.5)	(6.1)	(5.1)
Government budget										
Surplus or deficit (−), excluding grants[7]	−12.1	−10.2	−11.6	−10.2	−15.7	−16.8	−4.1	−8.2	−4.1	−3.9
Surplus or deficit (−), including grants[7]	−9.3	−6.0	−7.5	−4.7	−5.1	−7.2	1.8	−1.7	1.3	2.8
Revenue and grants	20.2	24.9	23.1	25.0	32.6	30.0	29.1	28.1	25.2	27.6
External sector										
Current account balance										
Excluding official transfers	−12.0	−18.2	−18.1	−16.5	−21.8	−16.0	−13.2	−18.1	−13.2	−13.9
Including official transfers	−1.5	−6.4	−3.3	−0.7	−2.1	3.9	1.9	−2.7	−0.1	0.3
External debt outstanding, including the IMF	96.3	108.9	118.5	112.9	122.6	122.6	101.4	87.7	82.0	85.6
	(In percent of net exports and travel income)[8]									
External debt service[9]										
Including the IMF	19.9	19.6	21.5	25.0	104.2	49.6	49.4	52.9	23.8	22.3
Excluding the IMF	16.7	16.4	12.5	15.0	71.0	38.0	41.6	45.6	16.4	17.8
	(In millions of SDRs)									
Current account balance										
Excluding official transfers	−27.1	−36.4	−34.9	−32.3	−35.8	−29.1	−27.8	−40.3	−32.3	−34.2
Including official transfers	−3.3	−12.7	−6.3	−1.3	−3.4	7.1	4.0	−6.0	−0.4	0.8
Overall balance of payments	−28.5	−18.5	−5.6	−11.6	25.8	13.7	5.1	20.1	21.1	23.1
External payments arrears *(end of period)*	20.5	51.0	57.4	88.2	41.8	32.2	14.2	0.2	—	—
Gross official reserves *(end of period)*	2.7	5.4	1.9	1.4	10.9	20.4	16.4	25.4	44.9	67.9
(in equivalent months of imports, c.i.f.)	0.4	0.6	0.3	0.2	1.4	2.6	1.7	2.1	3.4	4.9

Sources: Data provided by the Gambian authorities; and IMF staff estimates.
[1]Based on the revised national accounts statistics, which involve a significant upward adjustment in nominal GDP since 1981/82.
[2]Including re-export trade.
[3]Annual average data. For 1991/92 the data relate to the first eight months of the fiscal year.
[4]In percent of broad money at the beginning of the period.
[5]Data for 1991/92 relate to the rate prevailing as of April 1992.
[6]Gross national savings minus official transfers.
[7]Including special provisions.
[8]Net exports defined as total exports minus imports used for re-exports.
[9]Debt service paid, including cash payments for arrears reduction after 1985/86, and after debt relief.

Chart 3. External Developments

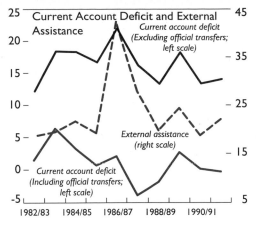

Current Account Deficit and External Assistance

Current account deficit
(Excluding official transfers;
left scale)

External assistance
(right scale)

Current account deficit
(Including official transfers;
left scale)

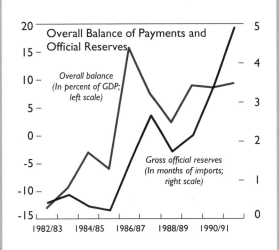

Overall Balance of Payments and Official Reserves

Overall balance
(In percent of GDP;
left scale)

Gross official reserves
(In months of imports;
right scale)

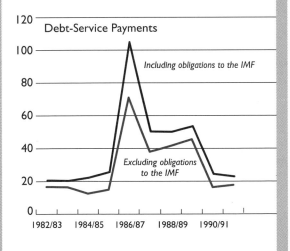

Debt-Service Payments

Including obligations to the IMF

Excluding obligations
to the IMF

Sources: Data provided by the Gambian authorities; and IMF staff estimates.
¹Inflows of official transfers and long–term concessional loans.

lion (less than a week of total imports) at the end of June 1986 to an estimated SDR 68 million at the end of June 1992, or the equivalent of 4.9 months of total imports.

The Gambia's external debt and debt-service position has also improved appreciably in recent years. As the arrears were being repaid, the external public debt declined from SDR 221 million (113 percent of GDP) at the end of June 1986 to SDR 196 million (88 percent of GDP) by the end of June 1990, before rising to an estimated SDR 211 million (86 percent of GDP) by the end of June 1992. Debt-service payments, on the other hand, inclusive of obligations to the Fund and of cash payments for arrears reduction and after debt relief, fell as a ratio of current foreign exchange earnings (i.e., domestic exports plus travel income and net re-exports) from a peak of 104 percent in 1986/87 to 22 percent by 1991/92. The external current account deficit in relation to GDP and the debt-service ratio are expected to continue to decline over the medium term, while gross official reserves are projected to rise further to more than five months of total imports. With the normalization of its relations with external creditors and the improvement in its external accounts achieved so far, The Gambia has reached a position where it no longer needs exceptional balance of payments financing, but continues to require sizable, though declining, inflows of foreign assistance in relation to GDP.

Notwithstanding the improvement in its economic and financial performance, The Gambia continues to be confronted with major structural, institutional, and financial constraints, as it remains highly vulnerable to adverse external developments and heavily dependent on foreign financial assistance. In addition, the country continues to face a number of deep-rooted developmental constraints, such as high population growth, underdeveloped human capital, paucity of natural resources, and degradation of the environment. These constraints are being addressed in the context of the country's ongoing reform efforts.

Table 3. Balance of Payments

	1982/83	1983/84	1984/85	1985/86	1986/87	1987/88	1988/89	1989/90	1990/91	1991/92 Est.
					(In millions of SDRs)					
Exports, f.o.b.	77.5	86.1	62.1	59.2	55.9	59.3	77.2	92.7	102.3	107.4
Of which: groundnuts	(22.8)	(31.7)	(15.9)	(8.5)	(9.8)	(13.5)	(13.2)	(12.9)	(11.1)	(10.2)
re-exports	(48.0)	(50.8)	(42.6)	(46.6)	(43.8)	(42.2)	(59.2)	(73.8)	(85.3)	(90.2)
Imports, f.o.b.	−81.7	−96.1	−74.9	−73.7	−78.6	−79.9	−98.4	−122.8	−136.6	−143.4
For domestic use	−54.4	−67.2	−50.6	−47.1	−53.6	−55.8	−63.4	−77.6	−84.4	−88.2
Of which: oil products	(...)	(...)	(...)	(−8.2)	(−5.6)	(−6.2)	(−5.7)	(−11.2)	(−16.5)	(−15.9)
For re-exports	−27.3	−28.9	−24.3	−26.6	−25.0	−24.1	−35.0	−45.2	−52.2	−55.2
Trade balance	−4.2	−10.0	−12.8	−14.5	−22.7	−20.6	−21.2	−30.1	−34.3	−36.0
Interest (net)	...	−6.2	−8.1	−12.6	−14.9	−10.4	−8.7	−9.0	−5.2	−5.5
Other services (net)	−27.1	−24.6	−18.6	−10.1	−4.3	−4.6	−3.9	−7.7	−1.1	−1.1
Of which: travel income	(14.2)	(18.4)	(18.5)	(20.6)	(27.5)	(28.0)	(31.4)	(30.4)	(39.7)	(41.1)
Private unrequited transfers (net)	4.2	4.4	4.6	4.8	6.0	6.6	6.0	6.5	8.4	8.5
Current account balance, excluding official transfers	−27.1	−36.4	−34.9	−32.3	−35.8	−29.1	−27.8	−40.3	−32.3	−34.2
Official unrequited transfers (net)	23.8	23.7	28.6	31.0	32.4	36.2	31.8	34.3	31.9	34.9
Current account balance, including official transfers	−3.3	−12.7	−6.3	−1.3	−3.4	7.1	4.0	−6.0	−0.4	0.8
Capital account	−25.2	9.5	5.7	−10.3	29.2	6.6	1.1	26.1	21.5	22.3
Official loans (net)	10.8	8.7	5.2	−4.6	28.5	6.5	0.4	10.3	6.0	10.2
Project loans	17.1	15.1	12.2	6.6	12.1	12.6	10.0	10.9	9.5	10.1
World Bank SACs[1]	—	—	—	—	25.0	1.7	—	9.2	4.4	9.4
Amortization	−6.3	−6.4	−7.0	−11.2	−8.6	−7.8	−9.6	−9.8	−7.9	−9.2
Private capital	−36.0	0.8	0.5	2.0	5.0	2.5	2.4	8.4	7.5	7.6
Short-term capital[2]	—	−15.3	−5.0	−7.7	−4.3	−2.4	−1.7	7.4	7.9	4.6
Overall balance	−28.5	−18.5	−5.6	−11.6	25.8	13.7	5.1	20.1	21.1	23.1
Financing	28.5	18.5	5.6	11.6	−25.8	−13.7	−5.1	−20.1	−21.1	−23.1
Gross official reserves (increase −)	1.6	−2.7	3.6	0.4	−9.5	−9.5	4.0	−9.0	−19.5	−23.4
Purchases/loans, IMF	8.8	2.6	—	—	11.2	7.2	6.8	6.8	3.4	3.4
Repurchases/repayments, IMF	−6.7	−0.7	−4.3	−9.1	−4.4	−4.2	−3.2	−3.1	−4.8	−3.1
Change in arrears (increase +)	24.8	19.3	6.4	20.3	−29.0	−6.9	−11.6	−14.8	−0.2	—
Exceptional financing[3]	—	—	—	—	3.0	1.5	—	—	—	—
Bank of England deposits[4]	—	—	—	—	2.9	−1.8	−1.1	—	—	—
Memorandum items										
Current account balance					*(In units indicated)*					
In percent of GDP[5]										
Excluding official transfers	−12.0	−18.2	−18.1	−16.5	−21.8	−16.0	−13.2	−18.1	−13.2	−13.9
Including official transfers	−1.5	−6.4	−3.3	−0.7	−2.1	3.9	1.9	−2.7	−0.1	0.3
Gross official reserves[6]										
In millions of SDRs	2.7	5.4	1.9	1.4	10.9	20.4	16.4	25.4	44.9	67.9
In months of total imports	0.4	0.6	0.3	0.2	1.4	2.6	1.7	2.1	3.4	4.9
Debt service[7,8]										
Including the Fund	19.9	19.6	21.5	25.0	104.2	49.6	49.4	52.9	23.8	22.3
Excluding the Fund	16.7	16.4	12.5	15.0	71.0	38.0	41.6	45.6	16.4	17.8

Sources: Data provided by the Gambian authorities; and IMF staff estimates.
[1] Structural adjustment credits; including cofinancing.
[2] Including private suppliers' credits and errors and omissions.
[3] Cash payments in connection with the Paris Club and London Club reschedulings.
[4] In respect of Paris Club rescheduling.
[5] Based on the revised GDP data.
[6] End of period.
[7] In percent of exports and travel income less imports used for re-exports.
[8] Including cash payments for arrears reduction, and after debt relief.

III Growth, Saving, and Investment

The growth potential of the Gambian economy has improved markedly since 1985/86 with the removal of distortions in the structure of relative prices, the strengthening in economic incentives, including the introduction of a market-determined exchange rate, and the rehabilitation of economic infrastructure. These policies have encouraged a diversification of the production base primarily toward services (such as regional trade and tourism) and to a lesser extent manufacturing, while broadening at the same time the base of agricultural output. Notwithstanding the progress made in diversifying economic activity, the output base of the economy remains fragile; it continues to be sensitive to changes in the weather, as well as external and regional developments.

The attainment of broad macroeconomic stability and the improved economic incentives have also contributed to a marked recovery in gross investment and domestically generated gross national savings from their low levels in 1985/86. The increase in gross investment was accompanied by an enhancement of its efficiency, particularly of government investment, thus supporting the strong expansion in output. The strengthening of the supply response of the economy facilitated the improvement in the savings performance, as well as in the external current account position, without undue restraint of domestic absorption. Notwithstanding the recovery in savings and investment in relation to GDP, savings and investment are still lower than their levels in the early 1980s and remain too modest to sustain a satisfactory expansion in economic growth and generate adequate employment opportunities for The Gambia's rapidly growing labor force. In view of this, the policies currently in place are aimed at stimulating private sector savings and investment, while strengthening further government finances and maintaining macroeconomic stability.

Developments in Output

Real GDP leveled off during the second half of the 1970s, but rose markedly in the early 1980s,

peaking in 1982/83, largely as a result of a steep expansion in groundnut production. Activity in agriculture fell sharply (26 percent) in the subsequent year, owing mainly to unfavorable weather, and recovered only modestly by 1985/86; this, together with a sluggish growth in industry and services, led to a similar trend in real GDP (Table 4). Following the introduction of the economic recovery program, real GDP grew steadily, at an annual average rate of 3.4 percent during the six-year period to 1991/92. During that time, real GDP growth was strongly influenced by the generally unfavorable weather and a marked decline in world groundnut prices, which led to a stagnation in agricultural output. The decline in real value added in agriculture was particularly strong in 1990/91, amounting to 14 percent, and despite an estimated increase of 5.4 percent in 1991/92, agricultural activity in that year was barely higher than in 1985/86. However, a marked expansion in real value added in the industrial and services sectors, averaging 4.5 percent and 4.1 percent a year, respectively, cushioned the adverse effects on total real GDP, thus facilitating a stabilization of real per capita income in the face of strong population growth. The Gambia's growth performance since 1985/86 compares favorably with the average for all sub-Saharan African countries, where it amounted on average to only 2.1 percent a year, significantly below the estimated annual rate of population growth (3 percent).[5]

Within the agricultural sector, a modest decline in real value added in crop production was offset by higher activity in the livestock, forestry, and fishery subsectors. Groundnut production fluctuated sharply from year to year, again owing largely to the vagaries of the weather and, in part, to a downward trend in real producer prices. In particular, after peaking at over 151,000 tons in 1982/83, groundnut production fell to 75,000 tons at the beginning of the adjustment efforts in 1985/86,

---

[5]For a review of recent trends in developing countries, see International Monetary Fund (1992).

Table 4. Gross Domestic Product by Kind of Economic Activity

	1982/83	1983/84	1984/85	1985/86	1986/87	1987/88	1988/89	1989/90	1990/91 Est.	1991/92 Est.
(In percent of real GDP)										
Agriculture	27.8	22.4	24.4	24.8	25.8	24.7	23.4	23.9	20.1	20.4
Crop Production	22.4	16.5	18.5	18.0	19.2	18.6	17.1	17.8	13.5	13.8
Of which: groundnuts	11.7	8.2	8.3	5.7	8.4	9.0	7.1	8.9	5.0	5.2
Livestock	3.8	4.1	4.0	4.4	4.3	4.5	4.5	4.5	4.5	4.5
Forestry	0.4	0.5	0.5	0.5	0.5	0.5	0.5	0.5	0.5	0.5
Fishing	1.1	1.3	1.4	1.8	1.8	1.1	1.3	1.1	1.6	1.5
Mining and quarrying	0.0	0.0	0.0	0.0	0.0	0.0	0.0	0.0	0.0	0.0
Industry	10.7	11.3	10.6	11.0	12.3	11.4	11.7	11.9	12.0	11.7
Manufacturing	6.0	5.7	4.4	5.5	5.9	6.7	6.3	6.1	5.8	5.5
Of which: groundnuts	0.9	0.3	0.2	0.2	0.3	0.3	0.3	0.5	0.1	0.0
Construction	4.4	5.2	5.8	5.1	5.9	4.1	5.0	5.3	5.6	5.7
Electricity	0.2	0.2	0.2	0.2	0.2	0.3	0.2	0.2	0.3	0.3
Water	0.2	0.2	0.2	0.2	0.2	0.2	0.2	0.2	0.3	0.3
Services	49.6	53.1	52.4	52.9	52.2	54.4	51.6	52.1	54.9	55.2
Trade	19.2	19.3	16.5	16.6	17.9	18.1	15.6	16.6	15.9	16.2
Of which: groundnut trade	8.0	7.1	4.0	3.5	3.3	4.2	1.6	2.9	1.8	1.8
Hotels and restaurants	2.1	3.1	3.5	3.9	3.6	3.7	3.7	3.2	4.2	4.4
Transport	6.1	8.1	8.9	8.3	9.1	9.5	8.2	8.1	8.7	8.6
Communications	0.8	0.9	1.0	1.3	2.0	3.5	4.3	5.0	6.4	6.6
Finance and insurance	1.9	0.2	0.6	2.7	3.4	3.2	3.0	3.0	3.4	3.4
Real estate and business services	5.7	6.4	6.3	6.4	6.3	6.2	6.2	6.1	6.1	6.1
Other services	1.7	1.9	2.0	2.0	2.0	2.0	2.0	2.0	2.0	2.0
Public administration	15.0	16.1	14.9	13.1	10.3	10.6	11.0	10.5	10.5	10.3
Less: imputed bank charges	3.0	2.8	1.3	1.5	2.3	2.4	2.4	2.4	2.4	2.4
GDP at factor cost	88.1	86.8	87.4	88.7	90.3	90.6	86.8	87.9	86.9	87.3
Indirect taxes (net)	11.9	13.2	12.6	11.3	9.7	9.4	13.2	12.1	13.1	12.7
GDP at constant prices	100.0	100.0	100.0	100.0	100.0	100.0	100.0	100.0	100.0	100.0
(Sectoral growth rates at constant prices; in percent)										
Agriculture		−26.0	10.5	5.8	7.0	−2.4	−1.2	7.3	−14.0	5.4
Corp Production		−32.6	13.8	1.8	9.4	−1.7	−4.1	10.0	−22.6	6.7
Of which: groundnuts		−35.4	2.7	−28.5	51.8	8.7	−18.0	32.1	−42.6	8.0
Livestock		−1.0	−1.4	13.7	0.1	7.3	4.8	3.6	3.6	3.0
Forestry		8.1	3.2	3.7	3.6	3.5	3.4	3.3	3.4	—
Fisheries		7.9	9.3	37.4	0.8	−35.7	20.7	−12.5	48.5	3.0
Mining and quarrying		3.3	3.2	3.7	3.6	3.5	3.4	3.3	10.0	—
Industry		−3.4	−4.1	8.0	14.7	−6.0	7.8	6.7	2.8	1.9
Manufacturing		−12.6	−21.2	29.4	11.7	15.0	−2.6	2.7	−3.3	−1.1
Of which: groundnuts		−64.7	−52.9	1.7	72.7	16.0	16.7	47.4	−69.8	−86.7
Construction		9.1	13.5	−8.5	18.5	−28.4	26.0	11.9	8.0	5.0
Electricity		3.5	2.5	13.4	10.1	13.9	−9.2	10.3	23.6	2.0
Water		−10.1	15.8	7.5	6.4	6.0	3.1	−0.7	22.7	2.0
Services		−1.7	0.2	5.1	1.4	6.1	−1.0	6.0	7.8	4.6
Trade		−8.0	−13.1	5.1	10.8	2.5	−10.1	12.0	−2.0	6.2
Of which: groundnuts		−19.3	−41.8	−10.8	−3.4	32.4	−60.6	88.5	−36.8	8.0
Hotels and restaurants		32.8	16.6	14.1	−4.2	5.1	4.8	−9.4	33.8	8.0
Transport		20.7	11.8	−2.0	11.8	6.4	−9.9	4.0	10.3	2.0
Communications		3.9	20.4	29.9	55.5	80.7	30.1	21.4	30.2	8.0
Finance and insurance		−88.0	145.1	383.8	26.4	−3.6	−1.4	4.6	17.5	2.0
Real estate and business services		1.9	1.2	5.5	0.6	1.0	3.0	3.5	2.6	4.0
Other services		3.2	3.8	4.5	3.2	4.3	3.7	6.8	1.5	2.0
Public administration		−1.6	−6.1	−8.2	−19.2	4.5	8.3	—	2.9	2.0
Less: imputed bank charges		−13.9	−53.2	19.5	62.8	4.1	4.6	5.7	2.8	2.0
GDP at factor cost		−9.6	2.3	5.7	4.6	2.0	0.0	6.5	1.2	4.4
Indirect taxes (net)		2.1	−2.9	−6.8	−11.4	−1.4	45.4	−3.3	10.4	1.2
GDP at constant market prices		−8.2	1.6	4.1	2.8	1.7	4.3	5.2	2.3	4.0

Sources: Data provided by the Gambian authorities; and IMF staff estimates.

before rising again to almost 130,000 tons in 1989/90. With a severe drought in 1990/91, groundnut production fell again to 74,000 tons and recovered only modestly to 84,000 tons in 1991/92. During the same period, groundnut oil prices in world markets displayed a pronounced year-on-year variability, falling overall from SDR 962 a ton in 1982/83 to SDR 565 a ton in 1991/92. As a consequence, the real producer price (purchase price since 1989/90) for groundnuts fluctuated as well, along a generally declining trend; by 1991/92, it was 27 percent lower than in 1982/83. The variability in groundnut production, together with changes in the producer price differential with a neighboring country,[6] has affected the quantity of groundnuts processed domestically by the GPMB, and thus activity in the manufacturing and trading sectors.

The services sector has benefited most from the improved macroeconomic environment and strengthened economic incentives, including the gains in external competitiveness. Within the services sector, strong increases have been recorded since 1985/86 in activity in the trade (including re-exports), tourism, transport and communications, and finance and insurance subsectors, amounting on an annual average basis to 4.9 percent, 5.5 percent, 11.5 percent, and 7.1 percent, respectively. The traditionally liberal trade regime maintained by The Gambia, combined with the lifting of exchange controls and the introduction of a market-determined exchange rate, boosted the expansion of re-exports to the subregion. Regional political developments have, on balance, also enhanced the importance of The Gambia as an entry point for regional trade. A broad range of basic consumer goods (such as rice, green tea, sugar, tomato paste, tobacco, footwear, and textiles) are usually imported into The Gambia, where they are sold wholesale to visiting traders from several neighboring countries. While the development of the re-export sector has had limited employment and income linkages to the rest of the economy, with the exception perhaps of the transport and communications and in part the banking sectors, it has had a major impact on foreign exchange earnings.

The Gambia's climate and sandy beaches offer an attractive and cheaper alternative to Mediterranean countries for many European tourists. As a result, the tourism sector has expanded markedly in recent years, aided in part by the fiscal incentives offered by the 1988 Development Act to domestic and foreign investors. The number of foreign-owned and -operated hotels has risen substantially, facilitating an increase in the number of tourists from 78,000 in 1985/86 to 109,000 in 1991/92, mainly under air charter tourist packages. While the import requirements of activity in the tourism sector remain fairly high, the strong expansion of the sector has boosted employment in the formal sector of the economy and activity in the construction sector, and has encouraged the development of related services, such as restaurants.

The industrial sector of The Gambia comprises mainly manufacturing and construction. Value added in the public utilities sector has traditionally been rather modest. Activity in the manufacturing sector has expanded on average by 3.5 percent a year since 1985/86, albeit from a low base. The development of the sector continues to be constrained by the small size of the economy, the limited availability of domestic raw materials, the frequent disruptions in the supply of electricity, and the weak managerial and technical expertise available in the country. Activity in the construction sector, on the other hand, has benefited from the emphasis of the public investment program on economic infrastructure and the construction of new hotels and of private houses for rent (mainly to expatriates).

The share of the industrial sector in total real GDP rose marginally from 11 percent in 1985/86 to 12 percent by 1991/92, while that of the services sector expanded from 53 percent to 55 percent, respectively. With the stagnation of activity in the agricultural sector, its share declined markedly, from 25 percent in 1985/86 (28 percent in 1982/83) to only 20 percent by 1991/92 (Chart 4). Although data on employment and the labor force are not available, it is believed that at least 60 percent of the labor force has traditionally been employed in the agricultural sector. The deteriorating income prospects in the rural areas have encouraged a high rate of urban migration, estimated at 6 percent a year. Although data are not available, it is estimated that the pace of employment generation in the urban areas may not have kept up with the rapidly increasing labor supply, resulting in increasing urban underemployment and unemployment.

Developments in Saving and Investment

Tentative estimates of saving and investment balances indicate that both gross investment and the domestically generated gross national savings

---

[6]Groundnut producer prices in Senegal have tended to be less sensitive to changes in the world market price for groundnuts, resulting in a generally sizable positive differential vis-à-vis producer prices in The Gambia (amounting to about 50 percent in 1991/92), which has encouraged cross border sales of groundnuts.

(i.e., excluding foreign grants) have recovered markedly from their low levels in 1985/86 (Table 5).[7] In particular, after declining from 10 percent of GDP in 1982/83 to a negative level equivalent to 1 percent of GDP in 1985/86, domestically generated savings rose to 5 percent of GDP by 1991/92. Similarly, gross national savings fell in relation to GDP from 22 percent in 1982/83 to 15 percent in 1985/86, before recovering to 19 percent by 1991/92.[8] Notwithstanding this recovery, both saving and investment in The Gambia are still too low to sustain a satisfactory growth in output, implying a continuing need to rely heavily on foreign savings (external current account deficit, excluding official transfers), as well as on foreign grants. While declining, the use of foreign savings by The Gambia and the value of foreign grants amounted each to the equivalent of 14 percent of GDP in 1991/92, a level not unduly high given The Gambia's stage of economic development.[9]

The expansion in domestic savings reflected contributions from both the government and private sectors, but the recovery in gross investment emanated entirely from the private sector (including the public enterprise sector). The improvement in the Government's savings performance, from 1 percent of GDP in 1985/86 to 3 percent in 1991/92, was associated with a decline in government investment as a ratio to GDP from 7 percent in 1985/86 (9 percent in 1982/83) to 5 percent in 1991/92. This resulted in a significant reduction in the Government's net financial deficit and contributed importantly to the strengthening of The Gambia's external current account position. It should be recognized, however, that while government investment declined relative to GDP, its efficiency has increased markedly through a more rigorous selection of investment projects and a greater emphasis on the rehabilitation of the basic economic infrastructure, thus supporting the recorded real GDP growth. The net financial deficit of the private sector, on the other hand, has been rather volatile. This reflected to a large extent the lumpi-

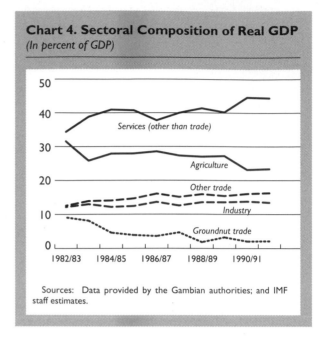

Chart 4. Sectoral Composition of Real GDP
(In percent of GDP)

Sources: Data provided by the Gambian authorities; and IMF staff estimates.

ness of investment projects undertaken in the late 1980s in the tourism sector and the tendency of private savings to change from year to year so as to cushion private consumption levels from the fluctuations in private disposable income caused by the swings in agricultural output and the external terms of trade. The still modest level of private savings reflects largely the low levels of real per capita incomes, the impact of the traditional extended family system, and, in part, the weak development of the domestic financial system, notwithstanding the restoration of positive real interest rates.[10] While data on the breakdown of private savings between personal and corporate savings are not available, it is believed that they comprise mainly profits by the business sector; part of these profits may have actually been placed abroad, given the absence of restrictions on capital movements and the foreign ownership of several enterprises in The Gambia, particularly in the tourism and trade sectors.

---

[7]The estimates of saving and investment balances are derived from partial indicators of sectoral expenditure patterns and thus, are unavoidably subject to a large margin for error.

[8]The Gambia's investment ratio compares favorably with that of other sub-Saharan African countries, which amounted to 17 percent of GDP in 1991, but is lower than the average for all developing countries (excluding Eastern Europe and the former U.S.S.R.), was estimated at 26 percent of GDP.

[9]To a large extent, the high level of foreign grants relative to GDP reflected sizable technical assistance.

[10]Although the empirical evidence suggests that interest rate policies have small effects on savings rates, maintenance of negative real interest rates for prolonged periods could lead to a flight out of financial savings. For a review of interest rate policies in developing countries, see International Monetary Fund (1983) and Aghevli and others (1990).

Table 5. National Income, Savings, and Investment
(In percent of GDP)

	1982/83	1983/84	1984/85	1985/86	1986/87	1987/88	1988/89	1989/90	1990/91 Est.	1991/92 Est.
GDP at market prices	100.0	100.0	100.0	100.0	100.0	100.0	100.0	100.0	100.0	100.0
GNP at market prices	100.0	96.9	95.8	88.5	85.5	89.2	91.4	91.6	94.0	93.9
Unrequited transfers, net[1]	12.4	14.1	17.2	18.3	23.4	23.6	17.9	18.3	16.5	17.6
Of which: official transfers	10.5	11.9	14.9	15.8	19.8	20.0	15.0	15.4	13.1	14.2
Gross disposable national income	112.4	111.0	113.0	106.8	108.9	112.8	109.3	109.9	110.5	111.5
Total consumption	91.6	94.7	95.1	92.1	91.4	93.3	89.9	92.0	91.4	92.2
Private consumption[2]	71.3	70.2	73.7	73.8	66.2	63.2	69.3	71.4	72.9	74.3
Government consumption[3]	20.2	24.5	21.5	18.3	25.2	30.1	20.6	20.6	18.5	17.9
Gross national savings	20.8	16.3	17.9	14.7	17.5	19.5	19.4	17.9	19.2	19.3
Government savings[4]	7.7	8.1	12.4	17.1	16.6	10.0	17.4	16.1	13.9	17.1
Private savings[2]	13.1	8.2	5.5	-2.4	0.9	9.4	2.0	1.8	5.3	2.2
Domestically generated savings[5]	10.3	4.4	3.0	-1.1	-2.3	-0.5	4.4	2.5	6.1	5.1
Gross domestic investment	22.3	22.7	21.2	15.4	19.6	15.5	17.6	20.6	19.3	19.0
Government investment[6]	9.3	9.7	11.9	7.1	6.9	6.7	5.3	5.1	5.1	5.3
Private investment[2]	13.0	13.0	9.3	8.2	12.6	8.8	12.3	15.5	14.2	13.7
External current account balance										
Including transfers	-1.5	-6.4	-3.3	-0.7	-2.1	3.9	1.9	-2.7	-0.1	0.3
Excluding transfers	-12.0	-18.2	-18.1	-16.5	-21.8	-16.0	-13.2	-18.1	-13.2	-13.9
Government financial balance[7]	-12.1	-13.5	-14.3	-5.9	-10.1	-16.6	-2.9	-4.4	-4.3	-2.3
Government savings[4]	-2.8	-3.8	-2.5	1.3	-3.2	-9.9	2.4	0.7	0.8	2.9
Government investment	9.3	9.7	11.9	7.1	6.9	6.7	5.3	5.1	5.1	5.3
Private financial balance[2,7]	0.1	-4.7	-3.8	-10.6	-11.7	0.6	-10.2	-13.7	-8.9	-11.5
Private savings	13.1	8.2	5.5	-2.4	0.9	9.4	2.0	1.8	5.3	2.2
Private investment	13.0	13.0	9.3	8.2	12.6	8.8	12.3	15.5	14.2	13.7

Sources: Data provided by the Gambian authorities; and IMF staff estimates.
[1] Consists of both official and private transfers.
[2] Includes public enterprises.
[3] Government current expenditure, less capital component of recurrent budget, plus current component of development budget.
[4] Domestic revenue (excluding capital revenue), less government consumption.
[5] Gross national savings, excluding official transfers.
[6] Development expenditure (excluding net lending), plus capital component of recurrent budget, less current component of development budget.
[7] Domestically generated financial balances.

IV   External Adjustment

An integral element of the Government's economic strategy has been the establishment of a market-determined exchange rate and the liberalization of the exchange and trade system. Both aspects were viewed as critical for strengthening economic incentives and achieving a viable balance of payments position.

Exchange Reform and Exchange Rate Policy

As indicated in Section II, the peg of the dalasi to the pound sterling was replaced in January 1986 with a flexible exchange rate system in the context of an interbank market. At the same time, the implementation of the Exchange Control Act was suspended, resulting essentially in the lifting of all the restrictions on current, as well as capital, international transactions. The liberalization of the exchange system was completed in July 1990, with the elimination by then of all the outstanding external payments arrears.[11]

Under the flexible exchange rate system, the exchange rate of the dalasi is determined freely by the supply and demand for foreign exchange between the authorized foreign exchange dealers and their customers, and among the dealers themselves (interbank market). Dealers are required to observe limits on their net holdings of foreign exchange, and amounts in excess of these limits have to be offered to the interbank market or sold to the Central Bank. The Central Bank holds a weekly fixing session with the participation of all foreign exchange dealers; the rate determined at this session is used mainly for statistical valuation purposes and applies only to transactions taking place at that time among the participants.[12] The

fixing sessions have also provided a forum for the dealers to exchange views on, and share assessments of, developments in the foreign exchange market. The number of authorized dealers was initially limited to the three commercial banks, but it has since been significantly increased, following the establishment of foreign exchange bureaus in April 1990. With the strong expansion of the re-export trade, the foreign exchange market has been deepened further, as a sizable volume of trade transactions in The Gambia is conducted in CFA francs.

The foreign exchange market has functioned fairly smoothly, resulting in the effective absorption of the parallel exchange market and a virtual elimination of the differential between the rates prevailing in the two markets; the spread has actually narrowed to less than 2 percent. Foreign exchange transactions between banks have tended to be modest, while transactions between authorized dealers and their customers have expanded substantially. Despite the lifting of controls on capital movements, the foreign exchange market in The Gambia has remained essentially a flow market, in the sense that supply and demand is linked more to current transactions rather than changes in the desired outstanding stocks of foreign exchange and dalasis (asset market). Nonetheless, it is estimated that the restoration of positive real interest rates on dalasi-denominated assets has encouraged currency substitution away from foreign exchange into domestic currency.

Exchange rate policy has focused on establishing and maintaining an appropriate market-determined exchange rate, so as to reverse the sizable overvaluation of the dalasi that had taken place prior to 1986 and thus stimulate the production and export of tradable goods. This has resulted in a major initial depreciation of the dalasi in real effective terms. The real effective exchange rate has since then been maintained broadly stable through appropriately restrictive fiscal and monetary policies, aimed at lowering inflation to a low level, comparable to the average for the main trading partner countries. Over the past couple of years,

---

[11]The provisions of the Exchange Control Act are not being implemented; it is expected that the Act will be repealed in the near future, following the envisaged enactment of a Revised Central Bank Act during the second half of 1992.

[12]For a detailed review of the functioning of flexible exchange rate systems introduced by developing countries in recent years, see Quirk and others (1987).

this emphasis of policies has facilitated a broadly stable nominal effective exchange rate of the dalasi as well. In this context, to support the exchange rate policy and help minimize the incentives for private capital outflows, interest rates in The Gambia have been maintained, through open market operations, at positive levels in real terms and with appropriate margins above interest rates abroad. These differentials have tended to be sizable, exceeding at times the inflation differentials and the ex post depreciation of the dalasi against the currencies of major industrial countries.[13] In May 1992, the treasury bill rate in The Gambia amounted to 18.5 percent, some 14.5, 8.0, and 8.5 percentage points higher than comparable instruments denominated in U.S. dollars, pounds sterling, and French francs, respectively.

The Central Bank does not intervene in the interbank market with a view to influence the movements in the exchange rate. However, it has tended to be a net purchaser of foreign exchange from the market so as to achieve quarterly quantitative targets for the level of gross official reserves, specified under the Government's adjustment program. For the most part, these purchases by the Central Bank have not had an undue impact on the prevailing exchange rate in the interbank market. On one occasion (in late 1990), however, when an unexpected decline in tourist arrivals and a disruption in the re-export trade affected adversely the supply of foreign exchange, the Central Bank's efforts to meet its gross reserve targets led to a marked depreciation of the dalasi.

Until mid-1990, the pace of accumulation of gross reserves by the Central Bank had been rather modest, given the need to gradually eliminate the outstanding external payments arrears. In particular, gross official reserves rose from the equivalent of less than a week of total imports in June 1986 to 2.1 months in June 1990, but have since then risen to an estimated 4.9 months of imports by June 1992, or 7.9 months of domestic imports. Such a level of reserve coverage is considered by the Government as necessary to facilitate the maintenance of a liberal exchange system, while providing a cushion against adverse exogenous shocks, given the country's vulnerability to changes in the weather, declines in the terms of trade, shortfalls in external assistance, and regional developments.

External Trade and Tariff Reform

The Gambia has traditionally maintained a liberal trade system, free of import quotas and other trade restrictions in the importation or exportation

---

[13]For a more detailed study of this issue, see Walsh (1991).

of any good other than groundnuts. The monopoly of the GPMB in the exportation of groundnuts was eliminated in January 1990. Since then, private traders have been allowed to use the processing facilities of the GPMB for the decortication of domestically purchased groundnuts for export. The Gambia's import tariff structure has tended to be lower than in neighboring countries, contributing to the development of the re-export trade. As part of the adjustment efforts since 1985/86, the tariff structure has been rationalized, with a view to achieving over time a low and uniform level of protection.

Soon after the introduction of a flexible exchange rate system in 1986, all specific import duties were converted into ad valorem equivalents. Moreover, the overall structure of customs duties has since been modified to avoid the excessive taxation of intermediate inputs and other anomalies, while average duty rates have been lowered. The general duty rate of 6 percent applied to all imports was eliminated following the introduction of a national sales tax in 1988, and the level of specific duties was reduced from an average of about 36 percent (excluding petroleum) in 1985/86 to about 20 percent by 1990/91. Most imports are now taxed at rates below 24 percent, with the major exceptions being petroleum products, motor vehicles, beer and alcohol, and soap. Beer and soap manufacturing are the only industries in The Gambia that are protected by relatively high import duties. Petroleum products are subject to a 10 percent sales tax, and a variable duty that is determined by the difference between the administered pump price, specific allowances to distributors, and the import costs. Currently, import duties on petroleum products range from about 170 percent to 250 percent. The 10 percent duty on exports of groundnut products was eliminated in 1989, thus reducing the vulnerability of the fiscal position to fluctuations in groundnut production, as well as improving production incentives to farmers. Tariff policy in The Gambia has also sought to encourage domestic trading activity by maintaining relatively low tariffs on commodities that are typically re-exported. In addition to the 10 percent sales tax, tariffs on these commodities generally range from zero to 10 percent.

Diversification of Exports

As highlighted in Sections II and III, strengthened economic incentives, particularly the establishment of a market-determined exchange rate and the associated gains in external competitiveness, together with the maintenance of a liberal trade regime and regional developments, have

Table 6. Foreign Exchange Earnings

	1982/83	1983/84	1984/85	1985/86	1986/87	1987/88	1988/89	1989/90	1990/91	1991/92 Est.
	(In millions of SDRs)									
Groundnuts	22.8	31.7	15.9	8.5	9.8	13.5	13.2	12.9	11.1	10.2
Other domestic exports	3.6	3.6	3.6	4.2	2.3	3.6	4.7	5.9	5.9	7.0
Net re-exports	17.1	17.0	14.2	15.5	14.6	14.1	18.4	21.1	24.4	25.8
Travel income	14.2	18.4	18.5	20.6	27.5	28.0	31.4	30.4	39.7	41.1
Total	57.7	70.7	52.2	48.8	54.3	59.2	67.7	70.4	81.1	84.1
	(Shares in the total; in percent)									
Groundnuts	39.5	44.9	30.4	17.4	18.1	22.8	19.5	18.4	13.7	12.1
Other domestic exports	6.2	5.1	6.9	8.6	4.3	6.1	7.0	8.4	7.3	8.3
Net re-exports	29.6	24.0	27.2	31.8	26.9	23.8	27.2	30.0	30.1	30.7
Travel income	24.6	26.0	35.4	42.2	50.7	47.3	46.4	43.2	48.9	48.8
Total	100.0	100.0	100.0	100.0	100.0	100.0	100.0	100.0	100.0	100.0

Sources: Data provided by the Gambian authorities; and IMF staff estimates.

Chart 5. Composition of Foreign Exchange Earnings, 1982/83–1991/92
(In percent of net exports plus travel income)

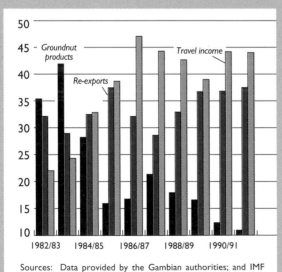

Sources: Data provided by the Gambian authorities; and IMF staff estimates.

given rise to a notable diversification of the production and export bases of the Gambian economy.

The strong expansion of the tourism sector has resulted in a doubling, between 1985/86 and 1991/92, of travel receipts, which have replaced groundnut exports as the most important source of foreign exchange earnings. At the same time, re-exports have become the second largest source of foreign exchange earnings. Other domestic exports (i.e., fish, cotton, and horticultural products) have also expanded markedly, albeit from a very low base. Consequently, the share of groundnuts in total foreign exchange earnings from domestic exports, net re-exports, and travel income declined from a peak of 45 percent in the early 1980s to an estimated 12 percent in 1991/92, while the shares of travel income and net re-exports rose from 24 percent and 26 percent to 49 percent and 31 percent, respectively (Chart 5 and Table 6).

V Fiscal Adjustment

In the decade to 1985/86, following the launching of The Gambia's first five-year development plan in 1975, public sector involvement in the economy increased substantially through the creation of public enterprises, the liberal provision of government-guaranteed loans at subsidized interest rates, and a large expansion in the size of the Central Government. Although a substantial increase in revenue mobilization occurred in this period, it was outpaced by a steep rise in expenditure, particularly with respect to the wage bill and public investment. The large increases in the wage bill reflected a doubling in the size of the civil service. In 1975, there were 4,000 civil servants and 2,000 nonpermanent staff. By 1985 these numbers had risen to 10,700 civil servants and 5,000 nonpermanent staff.

The large expansion in the size of the civil service, and the overly ambitious public investment program, contributed to a substantial deterioration in the fiscal position, which together with the exogenous shocks that hit The Gambian economy in the early 1980s, gave rise to mounting fiscal imbalances. The prolonged Sahelian drought of 1980–81 drastically affected government revenue, and the impact of the 1979 oil price hike and the rising inflation and interest rates in industrial countries further aggravated the domestic economic situation. In response, some cuts in current expenditure were effected, but the relatively high levels of public investment were maintained. This expenditure was increasingly financed by foreign borrowing, including substantial use of short-term loans. The overall fiscal deficit widened to the equivalent of 12 percent of GDP in 1982/83. As a result, the Government's inability to service its external debt obligations gave rise to a significant buildup of external payments arrears. Despite some improvement in revenue mobilization during the three-year period to 1985/86, the overall budget deficit was only contained by a sharp reduction in expenditure on operations and maintenance, which led to a deterioration in the physical infrastructure. By 1985/86, the fiscal deficit still exceeded 10 percent of GDP (Chart 6 and Table 7).

The ambitious public investment program, with the exception of investment in the tourism sector, reflected poor evaluation and selection of investment projects and contributed only marginally to raising the growth prospects of the economy. In addition, the creation of an inefficient public enterprise sector, together with prices administered at subsidized levels, led to the accumulation of large public enterprise debts to the domestic banking system, which will place a substantial burden on the fiscal position in subsequent years. For example, the external debt of several public enterprises has invariably been serviced by the Government.

These problems have been directly addressed in the context of the adjustment efforts pursued since 1985/86. An integral objective of these efforts has been a scaling back of the role of the public sector in the economy with a view to creating a favorable climate for private investment. To this end, fiscal policy has been aimed at lowering the budget deficit, raising government savings, and encouraging economic activity through tax reforms and more efficient public investment that has focused on developing the basic economic and social infrastructure. Fiscal policy has also played a role in alleviating the social impact of adjustment and of poverty in general.

Tax Policy

Tax policies during the period since 1985/86 have been directed at broadening the tax base, strengthening tax administration, and rationalizing the structure of taxation, so as to improve economic incentives and enhance the efficiency and equity of the tax system. These efforts have been aided by the positive impact on the tax base of the depreciation of the dalasi, the increasing volume of imports, and the rising level of economic activity. The key tax reforms implemented included a restructuring of customs duties, the repeal of export taxes, the introduction of a national sales tax, reductions in marginal tax rates on personal income, and increases in specific excise duties and charges.

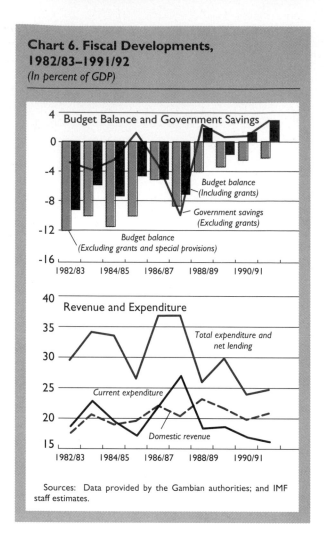

Chart 6. Fiscal Developments, 1982/83–1991/92
(In percent of GDP)

Budget Balance and Government Savings

Budget balance
(Including grants)

Government savings
(Excluding grants)

Budget balance
(Excluding grants and special provisions)

Revenue and Expenditure

Total expenditure and net lending

Current expenditure

Domestic revenue

Sources: Data provided by the Gambian authorities; and IMF staff estimates.

In the first two years of the adjustment efforts, domestic revenue benefited from the marked broadening of the tax bases, with tax reforms limited to a restructuring of import tariffs; as indicated in Section IV, all specific duties were converted into ad valorem rates, while the structure of customs duties was rationalized and the average duty rates lowered. Until 1987/88, the bulk of domestic revenue (over 70 percent) emanated from taxes on international trade (Table 8).

To reduce the reliance on this source of tax receipts, a national sales tax of 10 percent was introduced in 1988, applying to all goods produced or imported into The Gambia. Exemptions to the sales tax include goods for educational and religious purposes; foodstuffs other than wine, alcohol, and candies; production equipment; medical supplies; butane gas and gas cookers (for environmental reasons); packaging of goods for export; and air freight on exported Gambian pro-

duce. Since The Gambia has little domestic production of manufactured goods, the coverage of the sales tax has gradually been extended to cover most services, including the tourism industry. As a result, revenue from taxes on goods and services rose sharply, from 1 percent of GDP in 1987/88 to 6 percent of GDP in 1988/89 and to 8 percent of GDP in 1991/92; its share in total domestic revenue increased from 7 percent in 1987/88 to 40 percent in 1990/91, before easing to 36 percent in 1991/92, accompanied by a reduction in the share of taxes on international trade to 44 percent by 1991/92 (Chart 7). However, a substantial portion of domestic indirect tax receipts is still derived from international trade, as approximately 80 percent of taxes on goods and services is generated from the sales tax on imports.

Another key tax reform was a rationalization and restructuring of the personal income tax system with a view to improving private sector incentives. With effect from January 1, 1988, a standard deduction of D 5,000 has been introduced; marginal income tax rates have been lowered to a range of 10–35 percent (previously rates ranged from 2 percent to 75 percent), and the number of brackets has been reduced from 12 to 5; all income in kind has been made taxable; and stiffer provisions for enforcement have been established. The reforms of the income tax system have generally been revenue neutral, as taxes on income and property have remained at about 2.5–3.0 percent of GDP. Nontax revenue has also remained broadly constant in relation to GDP, while capital revenue has increased slightly, reflecting revenue generated from the divestiture of public enterprises.

Overall, the implementation of these tax reforms contributed to an increase in domestic revenue in relation to GDP from 20 percent in 1985/86 to a peak of 23 percent in 1988/89. Since then, however, domestic revenue declined steadily in relation to GDP, falling to 20 percent by 1991/92, largely as a result of the slowdown in the growth of economic activity, the impact of the reductions in customs duty rates on key commodities that feature prominently in the re-export trade (duty rates were reduced to zero for some commodities), and a widespread granting of discretionary customs duty waivers by the Government. In response to these developments, as well as to an overrun in current government expenditure in 1991/92, far-reaching reforms of customs duties and direct taxation began to be implemented in March 1992. The reforms were designed to strengthen tax administration, broaden the tax base, and further improve economic incentives. In particular, these reforms involved (1) the discontinuation of all discretionary and temporary customs duty waivers not

Table 7. Central Government Operations

	1982/83	1983/84	1984/85	1985/86	1986/87	1987/88	1988/89	1989/90	1990/91	1991/92 Est.
					(In millions of dalasis)					
Total revenue and grants	**122.4**	**153.6**	**180.8**	**271.8**	**484.7**	**490.1**	**565.3**	**659.6**	**678.5**	**860.1**
Revenue	105.6	127.6	148.5	212.7	328.3	333.5	450.5	508.4	533.3	650.5
Taxes on income and property	13.4	17.5	24.5	31.7	41.4	44.3	58.8	67.6	70.7	81.8
Taxes on goods and services	4.7	6.7	14.2	11.0	18.3	22.3	121.1	171.4	214.2	234.3
Taxes on international trade	73.5	91.1	97.4	147.8	245.4	234.8	228.6	217.1	235.2	289.5
Other taxes	0.2	0.4	0.5	0.5	0.7	0.9	1.2	1.1	1.2	1.1
Nontax revenue and capital revenue	13.8	12.0	11.9	18.9	22.1	27.2	35.9	43.6	−2.6	40.8
Foreign grants[1]	16.9	26.0	32.3	59.1	156.4	156.6	114.7	151.2	145.2	209.5
Total expenditure and net lending	**179.0**	**210.9**	**262.3**	**288.0**	**547.0**	**602.5**	**504.6**	**700.6**	**644.8**	**771.4**
Current expenditure	112.5	140.6	151.4	185.3	327.0	439.6	354.8	434.4	452.4	500.2
Personal emoluments, pensions, and allowances	52.9	55.1	58.9	63.1	64.7	71.4	101.6	133.3	144.8	153.0
Interest	11.7	17.3	29.2	38.2	75.5	66.9	85.3	95.3	104.5	108.8
Internal	. . .	. . .	18.2	16.2	26.6	19.1	23.3	42.6	50.3	57.6
External	. . .	. . .	11.0	22.0	48.9	47.9	62.0	52.7	54.2	51.2
Other charges	39.7	58.5	53.0	67.7	95.4	137.4	152.9	165.3	203.1	238.4
Goods and services	. . .	. . .	. . .	38.4	47.4	69.3	86.3	79.8	96.4	112.0
Maintenance and equipment	. . .	. . .	. . .	9.4	14.5	25.0	24.5	28.6	34.8	35.8
Subsidies and transfers	. . .	. . .	. . .	15.9	26.7	37.7	41.5	45.3	67.3	69.8
Other expenditure	. . .	. . .	. . .	4.0	6.8	5.5	0.7	11.5	4.6	20.8
Transfers to parastatals	8.2	9.8	10.2	16.3	91.4	163.9	15.0	40.5	—	—
Of which: The Gambia Produce Marketing Board	(1.2)	(. . .)	(0.4)	(12.4)	(83.0)	(130.7)	(13.2)	(40.5)	(—)	(—)
Development expenditure and net lending	66.5	70.3	109.1	94.8	221.8	173.4	138.8	262.1	194.9	266.6
Development expenditure	66.5	70.3	109.1	91.1	153.3	176.1	141.1	173.0	198.3	216.0
Net lending	—	—	—	3.7	68.5	−2.7	−2.3	89.1	−3.4	50.6
Of which: Managed Fund	(—)	(—)	(—)	(—)	(72.6)	(−2.7)	(−2.3)	(−2.4)	(−1.1)	(−1.4)
Unallocated expenditure	—	—	1.9	7.9	−1.8	−10.6	11.0	4.1	−2.5	4.6
Change in arrears (decrease −)	—	20.5	23.2	−35.0	−14.1	−5.4	−25.5	—	—	—
Surplus or deficit (−)										
Excluding foreign grants	−73.5	−62.8	−90.6	−110.3	−232.8	−274.4	−79.6	−192.2	−111.5	−120.9
Excluding foreign grants and special provisions[2]	−73.5	−62.8	−90.6	−110.3	−77.2	−143.7	−79.6	−81.2	−68.1	−69.9
Including foreign grants	−56.6	−36.8	−58.3	−51.2	−76.4	−117.8	35.1	−41.0	33.7	88.6
Financing	56.6	36.8	58.3	51.2	76.4	117.8	−35.1	41.0	−33.7	−88.6
Foreign (net)	31.2	21.2	38.0	7.1	241.4	73.8	14.5	116.4	91.1	163.3
Borrowing	36.7	32.1	59.9	36.6	301.0	129.1	91.4	209.5	154.1	242.7
Repayments	−5.5	−10.9	−21.9	−29.5	−64.2	−60.4	−76.9	−93.1	−63.0	−79.4
Domestic	25.4	15.6	20.3	44.1	−165.0	44.0	−49.7	−75.4	−124.8	−251.9
Banking system	23.7	5.4	14.5	20.4	−165.0	27.4	−77.7	−0.1	−164.1	−302.0
Nonbank	1.7	10.2	5.8	23.7	—	20.1	31.6	−6.3	44.3	50.0
Sinking fund for debt relief	—	—	—	—	—	−3.5	−3.5	−69.0	−5.0	—
					(In percent of GDP)[3]					
Domestic revenue	17.4	20.7	19.0	19.6	22.1	20.4	23.2	21.7	19.8	20.9
Total expenditure and net lending	29.6	34.1	33.6	26.5	36.8	36.8	26.0	29.9	24.0	24.7
Surplus or deficit (−)										
Excluding foreign grants	−12.1	−10.2	−11.6	−10.2	−15.7	−16.8	−4.1	−8.2	−4.1	−3.9
Excluding foreign grants and special provisions	−12.1	−10.2	−11.6	−10.2	−5.2	−8.8	−4.1	−3.5	−2.5	−2.2
Including foreign grants	−9.3	−6.0	−7.5	−4.7	−5.1	−7.2	1.8	−1.7	1.3	2.8

Sources: Data provided by the Gambian authorities; and IMF staff estimates.

[1] Foreign grants correspond to official unrequited transfers in the balance of payments less technical assistance grants.

[2] Special provisions consist of D 72.6 million for the creation of the Managed Fund and D 83.0 million in budgetary support for the GPMB in 1986/87, D 130.7 million for budgetary support for the GPMB in 1987/88, D 111.0 million for the liquidation of public enterprise debt in 1989/90, D 43.4 million for the covering of the Central Bank's losses in 1990/91, and an estimated D 51.0 million for the replacement of the net nonperforming assets of the The Gambia Commercial and Development Bank in 1991/92.

[3] Based on the revised GDP data.

Table 8. Structure of Government Revenue

	1985/86	1986/87	1987/88	1988/89	1989/90	1990/91	1991/92 Est.
			(In percent of GDP)				
Domestic revenue	19.6	22.1	20.4	23.2	21.7	19.8	20.9
Tax revenue	17.6	20.6	18.5	21.1	19.5	19.4	19.5
Taxes on income and property	2.9	2.8	2.7	3.0	2.9	2.6	2.6
Taxes on goods and services	1.0	1.2	1.4	6.2	7.3	8.0	7.5
Taxes on international trade	13.6	16.5	14.4	11.8	9.3	8.7	9.3
Other taxes	—	—	0.1	0.1	—	—	—
Nontax revenue	1.7	1.5	1.7	1.8	1.9	−0.1	1.3
Capital revenue	0.3	—	0.2	0.2	0.3	0.5	0.1
Foreign grants	5.4	10.5	9.6	5.9	6.4	5.4	6.7
Total revenue and grants	25.0	32.6	30.0	29.1	28.1	25.2	27.6
			(In percent of total domestic revenue)				
Tax revenue	89.8	93.2	90.6	91.0	89.9	97.7	93.3
Taxes on income and property	14.9	12.6	13.3	13.1	13.3	13.2	12.6
Taxes on goods and services	5.1	5.6	6.7	26.9	33.7	40.2	36.0
Taxes on international trade	69.5	74.8	70.4	50.8	42.7	44.1	44.5
Other taxes	0.2	0.2	0.3	0.3	0.2	0.2	0.2
Nontax revenue	8.9	6.7	8.1	8.0	8.6	−0.5	6.3
Capital revenue	1.3	0.1	1.2	1.1	1.5	2.8	0.5
Total domestic revenue	100.0	100.0	100.0	100.0	100.0	100.0	100.0

Sources: Data provided by the Gambian authorities; and IMF staff estimates.

explicitly provided for under the 1988 Development Act or by international agreements (e.g., for diplomats and project-related imports financed by donors); (2) a stricter monitoring of the concessions granted under the Development Act; (3) a tightening of the arrangements for "direct delivery" of imported goods, under which the payment of customs duties can be deferred for specified periods; (4) a rationalization of the customs clearing procedures, including computerization, so as to eliminate anomalies and the potential for abuse; and (5) the preparation by the Commissioner of Income Tax of more rigorous assessments of the turnover and tax liability of individual corporations. While the full effects of these measures would be felt over time, some improvement in tax collections has already been evidenced in the last quarter of 1991/92.

Expenditure Policy

Within the context of a strategy designed to reduce the overall fiscal deficit, expenditure policies since 1985/86 have been aimed at lowering total expenditure and net lending in relation to GDP, as well as at changing the composition of total government spending in favor of outlays on the priority areas. In this regard, the primary focus of the adjustment efforts has been to reduce the relative size of the civil service wage bill, eliminate the substantial implicit and explicit transfers to public enterprises, and improve the efficiency of public investment, in order to increase budgetary provisions for operations and maintenance, the social sectors, and investment on the rehabilitation and development of the basic economic and social infrastructure.

These policies have succeeded in reducing total expenditure and net lending as a proportion of GDP from 27 percent in 1985/86 to an estimated 25 percent by 1991/92 (Table 9). During some of the intervening years, however, expenditure rose sharply. In 1986/87 and 1987/88, it reached a peak of 37 percent of GDP, when the Government took over nonperforming bank loans and made provisions for the liquidation of public enterprise debt. The composition of expenditure also changed in this period: personal emoluments, transfers to parastatals, and development expenditure and net lending all declined as a proportion of GDP. In particular, the locally financed component of development expenditure was reduced from 4 percent of GDP in 1985/86 to 1 percent of GDP in the subsequent years. On the other hand, expenditure on "other charges" rose from 6 percent of GDP in 1985/86 to 8 percent in 1991/92, reflecting, in part, increased provisions for operations and maintenance and the social sectors.

The principal reform initiated at the outset of the adjustment efforts was a restructuring of the civil service pay and employment structure, with World Bank support. The first stage took place in early 1986 and involved the removal of 2,600 temporary workers (out of a total of 5,000), a reduction in the budgetary provision for vacant posts to token amounts, and the elimination of the practice of transferring funds from other expenditure categories to wages and salaries.[14] The second stage, instituted in August 1986, involved the retrenchment of 900 civil servants (about 9 percent of the total), the addition of 300 temporary staff, and the elimination of 800 vacancies from the roster of established posts. Since the completion of the retrenchment exercise, the Government has attempted to keep the overall size of the civil service broadly constant; however, control of civil service employment has not always been adequate, and staffing levels have increased in certain years. At the end of December 1991, the number of established posts in the civil service stood at about 9,500, or some 11 percent lower than in 1985. Within a declining total, the number of teachers was raised markedly, so as to prevent increases in, if not lower, the already high pupil-to-teacher ratio in the face of rising school enrollments.

During the implementation of the retrenchment program, and while a pay and grading exercise was being carried out, civil service salaries were frozen. The change to a new grade structure, which reduced the number of grades from 19 to 12, took place in October 1988, and a general pay increase of 67 percent was awarded in January 1989—the first pay increase in the civil service since July 1985. Following this discrete adjustment, there were no further increases in civil service salaries until July 1991, when a 6 percent increase was awarded. As a consequence, the growth in average wage earnings has not kept up with the increase in consumer

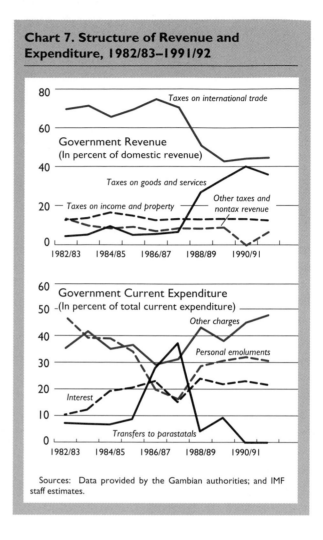

Chart 7. Structure of Revenue and Expenditure, 1982/83–1991/92

Sources: Data provided by the Gambian authorities; and IMF staff estimates.

prices, undermining efforts to attract and retain skilled civil servants. Current government pay policy calls for annual increases in civil service wages based on the targeted average rate of inflation, the need to attract and retain qualified personnel, overall productivity gains in the economy, and the availability of domestic budgetary resources.

The civil service reform program in The Gambia was implemented relatively quickly and efficiently in comparison with the experience of some other West African countries.[15] But a bigger challenge has been to follow through on the short-term gains by developing a small, productive, and highly motivated civil service. This objective remains elusive, and the Government continues to have problems recruiting and retaining qualified personnel.

---

[14]Budgetary provisions are based on established posts and therefore include provisions for vacant posts. The process of transferring funds from other expenditure categories to wages and salaries was eliminated in order to prevent expenditure savings from elsewhere in the budget being used to hire additional temporary workers.

---

[15]For a comparison of the experience with civil service reform of The Gambia, Ghana, and Guinea, see de Merode (1991). For a comprehensive review of Ghana's adjustment efforts, see Kapur and others (1991).

Table 9. Structure of Government Expenditure

	1985/86	1986/87	1987/88	1988/89	1989/90	1990/91	1991/92 Est.
				(In percent of GDP)			
Current expenditure	17.1	22.0	26.9	18.3	18.5	16.8	16.0
Personal emoluments, pensions, and allowances	5.8	4.4	4.4	5.2	5.7	5.4	4.9
Interest due	3.5	5.1	4.1	4.4	4.1	3.9	3.5
Internal	1.5	1.8	1.2	1.2	1.8	1.9	1.8
External	2.0	3.3	2.9	3.2	2.2	2.0	1.6
Other charges	6.2	6.4	8.4	7.9	7.0	7.6	7.6
Goods and services	3.5	3.2	4.2	4.4	3.4	3.6	3.6
Maintenance and equipment	0.9	1.0	1.5	1.3	1.2	1.3	1.1
Subsidies and transfers	1.5	1.8	2.3	2.1	1.9	2.5	2.2
Other expenditure	0.4	0.5	0.3	—	0.5	0.2	0.7
Transfers to parastatals	1.5	6.2	10.0	0.8	1.7	—	—
Development expenditure and net lending	8.7	14.9	10.6	7.1	11.2	7.2	8.6
Development expenditure	8.4	10.3	10.8	7.3	7.4	7.4	6.9
Net lending	0.3	4.6	-0.2	-0.1	3.8	-0.1	1.6
Total expenditure and net lending	26.5	36.8	36.8	26.0	29.9	24.0	24.7
			(In percent of total expenditure and net lending)				
Current expenditure	64.3	59.8	73.0	70.3	62.0	70.2	64.8
Personal emoluments, pensions, and allowances	21.9	11.8	11.8	20.1	19.0	22.5	19.8
Interest due	13.3	13.8	11.1	16.9	13.6	16.2	14.1
Internal	5.6	4.9	3.2	4.6	6.1	7.8	7.5
External	7.6	8.9	7.9	12.3	7.5	8.4	6.6
Other charges	23.5	17.4	22.8	30.3	23.6	31.5	30.9
Goods and services	13.3	8.7	11.5	17.1	11.4	15.0	14.5
Maintenance and equipment	3.3	2.7	4.1	4.9	4.1	5.4	4.6
Subsidies and transfers	5.5	4.9	6.3	8.2	6.5	10.4	9.1
Other expenditure	1.4	1.2	0.9	0.1	1.6	0.7	2.7
Transfers to parastatals	5.6	16.7	27.2	3.0	5.8	—	—
Development expenditure and net lending	32.9	40.5	28.8	27.5	37.4	30.2	34.6
Development expenditure	31.6	28.0	29.2	28.0	24.7	30.8	28.0
Net lending	1.3	12.5	-0.4	-0.5	12.7	-0.5	6.6
Total expenditure and net lending	100.0	100.0	100.0	100.0	100.0	100.0	100.0

Sources: Data provided by the Gambian authorities; and IMF staff estimates.

While adequate control on total government expenditure has broadly been established since 1985/86, difficulties in controlling certain expenditure items that are centrally administered (other than the wage bill, such as external travel) continued for some time, necessitating expenditure cuts in other areas of current spending.[16] This has meant that the Ministries of Health and Education, among others, have been held for some years below their budgetary allocations. These problems have been addressed during the last three years and the situation has improved considerably. Given the importance attached by the Government to developing human capital, and notwithstanding the pursuit of continued fiscal adjustment, the budgetary allocations for improvements in the quality of social services have been significantly increased; in particular, the combined share of recurrent outlays on education and health in total current spending (excluding interest payments), after having declined from 27 percent in 1985/86 to 13 percent

[16]Similarly, during the early 1980s, the pressures of the deteriorating economic and financial environment led to reductions in expenditure in areas where effective political interest groups could not be formed to protect their budgetary allocations. As a result, expenditure reductions tended to affect outlays on operations and maintenance and to some extent recurrent spending on health and education.

Table 10. Functional Classification of Current Expenditure by Key Ministries

	1985/86	1986/87	1987/88	1988/89	1989/90	1990/91	1991/92 Budget
	(In millions of dalasis)						
Office of the President	11.1	10.5	22.0	28.8	36.3	34.8	31.3
Ministry of Agriculture	10.7	9.4	13.3	14.5	14.3	17.4	19.3
Ministry of Works and Communications	11.2	10.2	15.0	16.8	16.7	18.2	13.8
Ministry of Education, Youth, Sports, and Culture	24.2	24.8	28.4	44.3	60.8	71.1	76.8
Ministry of Health, Labor, and Social Welfare	14.7	17.9	20.7	25.4	30.2	34.8	38.9
Ministry of Defense	5.9	8.6	11.1	17.9	23.4	31.2	36.3
Ministry of External Affairs	6.9	13.2	19.3	21.7	21.6	24.6	25.0
Other	62.3	157.0	242.9	100.2	135.8	115.8	123.5
Total current expenditure[1]	147.0	251.6	372.7	269.5	339.1	347.9	365.0
	(In percent of current expenditure)						
Office of the President	7.5	4.2	5.9	10.7	10.7	10.0	8.6
Ministry of Agriculture	7.3	3.7	3.6	5.4	4.2	5.0	5.3
Ministry of Works and Communications	7.6	4.1	4.0	6.2	4.9	5.2	3.8
Ministry of Education, Youth, Sports, and Culture	16.5	9.9	7.6	16.4	17.9	20.4	21.0
Ministry of Health, Labor, and Social Welfare	10.0	7.1	5.6	9.4	8.9	10.0	10.7
Ministry of Defense	4.0	3.4	3.0	6.6	6.9	9.0	9.9
Ministry of External Affairs	4.7	5.2	5.2	8.1	6.4	7.1	6.9
Other	42.4	62.4	65.2	37.2	40.1	33.3	33.8
Total current expenditure	100.0	100.0	100.0	100.0	100.0	100.0	100.0

Sources: Data provided by the Gambian authorities; and IMF staff estimates.
[1]Government current expenditure excluding interest.

in 1987/88, was raised steadily to 32 percent by 1991/92 (Table 10).

Government transfers to public enterprises and net lending have been strongly influenced by the Government's groundnut pricing policy and the reform efforts in the public enterprise and financial sectors. As indicated in Section II, producer prices for groundnuts were deliberately set high in the early stages of adjustment, so as to encourage a reversal of cross-border sales of groundnuts, thus necessitating sizable budgetary subsidies to the GPMB to cover its operating costs during 1986/87 and 1987/88. Similarly, as part of the efforts to restructure certain key public enterprises and improve their financial performance, the financial liabilities of these enterprises to the state-owned commercial bank (the GCDB) were repaid by the Government in 1989/90, thus boosting the budgetary provisions for net lending in that year. In addition, in the context of the efforts to restructure the GCDB and prepare it for privatization, the Government took over in 1986/87 the GCDB's nonperforming loans to other public enterprises that had been guaranteed by the Government, as well as the remaining nonperforming loans (net of GCDB's liquid assets) in late 1991/92. Finally, the budget for 1990/91 provided for special transfers to the Central Bank to cover its operating losses sustained in earlier years; thereafter, the Central Bank's net profit position was explicitly incorporated in the budget as part of nontax receipts. As a result of these special provisions, the outlays on government subsidies to public enterprises and net lending fluctuated markedly from year to year. In particular, subsidies to public enterprises rose from 1.5 percent of GDP in 1985/86 to a peak of 10 percent in 1987/88 but were brought down to zero by 1990/91.

Further improvements in the budgetary procedures are expected in the period ahead as a result of the ongoing work to develop public expenditure

Table 11. Alternative Measures of the Budget Balance
(In percent of GDP)

	1982/83	1983/84	1984/85	1985/86	1986/87	1987/88	1988/89	1989/90	1990/91	1991/92 Est.
Total revenue and grants	20.2	24.9	23.1	25.0	32.6	30.0	29.1	28.1	25.2	27.6
Revenue	17.4	20.7	19.0	19.6	22.1	20.4	23.2	21.7	19.8	20.9
Of which: capital revenue	...	...	...	0.3	0.0	0.2	0.2	0.3	0.5	0.2
Foreign grants	2.8	4.2	4.1	5.4	10.5	9.6	5.9	6.4	5.4	6.7
Total expenditure and net lending	29.6	34.1	33.6	26.5	36.8	36.8	26.0	29.9	24.0	24.7
Current expenditure	18.6	22.8	19.4	17.1	22.0	26.9	18.3	18.5	16.8	16.0
Of which: interest	1.9	2.8	3.7	3.5	5.1	4.1	4.4	4.1	3.9	3.5
Development expenditure	11.0	11.4	14.0	8.4	10.3	10.8	7.3	7.4	7.4	6.9
Of which: locally financed	...	...	...	3.7	0.9	1.0	1.1	0.9	1.0	0.9
Net lending	—	—	—	0.3	4.6	-0.2	-0.1	3.8	-0.1	1.6
Unallocated expenditure	—	—	0.2	0.7	-0.1	-0.6	0.6	0.2	-0.1	0.1
Change in arrears (decrease −)[1]	—	3.3	3.0	-3.2	-0.9	-0.3	-1.3	—	—	—
Overall balance (−)										
Excluding foreign grants	-12.1	-10.2	-11.6	-10.2	-15.7	-16.8	-4.1	-8.2	-4.1	-3.9
Excluding foreign grants and special provisions[2]	-12.1	-10.2	-11.6	-10.2	-5.2	-8.8	-4.1	-3.5	-2.5	-2.2
Including foreign grants	-9.3	-6.0	-7.5	-4.7	-5.1	-7.2	1.8	-1.7	1.3	2.8
Current budget balance[3]										
Excluding grants	...	...	...	2.3	0.1	-6.7	4.7	2.8	2.5	4.7
Including grants	...	...	...	7.7	10.6	2.8	10.6	9.3	7.9	11.4
Primary budget balance[4]										
Excluding grants	-10.2	-10.7	-10.8	-3.4	-9.6	-12.4	1.6	-4.1	-0.3	-0.4
Including grants	-7.4	-6.5	-6.7	2.0	0.9	-2.8	7.5	2.3	5.1	6.3
Primary budget balance[5]										
Excluding grants	...	...	...	2.3	4.2	-3.4	8.2	6.4	5.9	7.4
Including grants	...	...	...	7.8	14.8	6.2	14.1	12.8	11.3	14.2

Sources: Data provided by the Gambian authorities; and IMF staff estimates.

[1] Represents the repayment of government external payments arrears.

[2] For a breakdown of special provisions see Table 7, footnote 2.

[3] Total revenue, minus capital revenue, less current expenditure.

[4] Total revenue, minus total expenditure and net lending (excluding interest).

[5] Total revenue, minus current expenditure (excluding interest), net lending, and the locally financed portion of development expenditure.

programs in key ministries. In this context, public expenditure programs were completed in 1991/92 for the priority sectors of education, health, agriculture, and public works and communication. It is envisaged that the public expenditure programs would be updated and rolled forward on an annual basis; their coverage would be broadened to cover all expenditure categories, thus facilitating greater consistency between the public investment program and the outlays for operations and maintenance provided for in the recurrent budget.

During the adjustment period, the Government has made use of a three-year rolling public investment program, which has emphasized the need to provide adequate infrastructure and support services for the development of the private sector and the promotion of human resource development. Public investment thus has focused on infrastructure (transport, communications, and public utilities), agriculture and natural resources, health, and education. The public investment program for each year is established taking into account resource availability, debt-servicing capacity, and the overall stance of fiscal policy. In collaboration with the World Bank, selection criteria for investment projects have been developed with a view to increasing the efficiency of public investment. These criteria entail (1) the completion of an adequate feasibility study; (2) the prospect of attaining an economic rate of return (where calculable) of at least 15 percent (projects in the social sectors, where an economic rate of return cannot be determined, are selected on the basis of least cost alternatives); (3) compatibility of the recurrent cost implications with future recurrent budgets; and (4) compatibility with medium-term balance of payments objectives. The increased rigor in project selection has also helped to mobilize external financial support for public investment; the share of the

development budget financed by local resources has fallen significantly since 1985/86.

Developments in the Budget Balance

Overall, the budget deficit (excluding foreign grants) widened initially from 10 percent of GDP in 1985/86 to a peak of 17 percent in 1987/88, but has since declined to an estimated 4 percent of GDP by 1991/92. The evolution of the budget deficit has been strongly influenced by the impact of the special provisions indicated above, which have masked the extent of the underlying improvement in the fiscal position achieved through the expenditure and tax policies pursued since 1985/86. Excluding these special provisions, as well as foreign grants, the budget deficit declined fairly steadily from 10 percent of GDP in 1985/86 to an estimated 2.2 percent by 1991/92. The budget for 1992/93 provides for a further reduction in the deficit to 2 percent of GDP.

The substantial strengthening in the fiscal position since 1985/86 is also illustrated by the evolution of other measures of the budget deficit. In particular, the current budget surplus, excluding grants, increased from 2.3 percent of GDP in 1985/86 to 4.7 percent by 1991/92 (Table 11), consistent with an increase in government savings (on a national accounts basis) from 1.3 percent of GDP to 2.9 percent, respectively (Table 5). More important, the primary budget surplus, excluding foreign grants and the externally financed portion of development expenditure, rose from 2.3 percent of GDP to 7.5 percent. Overall, despite the severity of the fiscal imbalances at the onset of the adjustment efforts, the relatively quick introduction of several key adjustment measures paved the way for the restoration of a fiscal position consistent with a stable overall macroeconomic framework.

VI Monetary Policy and Financial Sector Reform

Monetary policy since the inception of The Gambia's Economic Recovery Program has been directed at (1) reducing inflation, which had accelerated sharply in 1984/85 and 1985/86; (2) replenishing the country's foreign exchange reserves from their initial very low level; (3) supporting the exchange rate policy; and (4) accommodating the targeted expansion in real GDP.

Monetary Policy Objectives and Instruments

Consistent with the targeted accumulation of gross official reserves and the large inflows of external financial assistance envisaged under the program, the expansion of broad money throughout the period since 1985/86 has been programmed to reflect an improvement in the net foreign assets of the banking system, while the net domestic assets of the banking system have been targeted to decline steadily. This reduction was to be achieved through large net repayments by the Government to the banking system, which would also make room for an adequate expansion of credit to the nongovernment sector, within the context of a restrictive overall credit policy.

Given the limited development of the domestic money market during the early years of the program, the Government has unavoidably relied on direct policy instruments—namely, quantitative controls on credit expansion by individual banks—for influencing credit and monetary developments and thus observing the ceilings on the net domestic assets of the banking system, net credit to the Government, credit to the GPMB, and the floors on the gross official reserves of the Central Bank (in foreign currency terms). However, to enhance the efficiency of monetary control and, in particular, to support the exchange rate policy and encourage domestic financial savings, the controls on bank deposit and lending interest rates were lifted in September 1985, including the discontinuation of subsidized lending rates for crop financing;[17] the bank cash-reserve requirements have been tightened;[18] and an auction market for treasury bills was introduced in July 1986. After the Central Bank had gained experience and confidence in managing domestic liquidity, the system of credit ceilings was abolished and an indirect system of monetary control was introduced with effect from September 1990.[19] Since then, the Central Bank has been exercising control over credit and monetary developments by observing limits on its net domestic assets and by maintaining tight domestic liquidity conditions through open market operations.

In its liquidity management policy, throughout the period since 1985/86, the Central Bank has been aiming to ensure that domestic interest rates were kept at levels that were positive in real terms and that appropriate differentials were maintained from interest rates abroad. Such a policy was considered essential for the smooth functioning of the interbank foreign exchange market, given the lifting of all exchange restrictions, including for capital transactions, and the large foreign exchange flows associated with the re-export trade.

Monetary policy reforms have been complemented by parallel efforts to strengthen the financial intermediation process. These efforts have focused initially on the restructuring and eventual

---

[17]The only control on interest rates that has been retained relates to a requirement that bank interest rates on three-month deposits be set at 3 percentage points below the prevailing interest rate on treasury bills, so as to ensure that the returns on bank deposits do not become too low.

[18]In September 1985, the required bank cash-reserve ratio was raised from 6 percent to 10 percent for demand deposits and from 4 percent to 8 percent for time and savings deposits. In 1986/87, the required cash-reserve ratio for demand deposits was raised further to 24 percent, while the required total liquid assets (including bank cash reserves) were raised to the equivalent of 30 percent of total bank deposits.

[19]The Gambia was the first sub-Saharan African country to shift to an indirect system of monetary control. Malawi and Ghana introduced a similar system in January 1991 and January 1992, respectively.

privatization of the largest commercial bank, the GCDB, which had been experiencing financial difficulties (including a large portfolio of nonperforming loans). More recently, attention has been directed at improving bank supervision and revising the financial sector legislation.

Monetary Developments Since 1985/86

Monetary policy during the period since 1985/86 has been broadly successful in reducing inflation, stabilizing the exchange rate, and facilitating the attainment of the real GDP and balance of payments objectives. As indicated in Section II, deviations from the initial program targets for these variables and the intermediate targets for monetary aggregates have been caused primarily by exogenous factors—such as weather developments, regional disturbances, and shortfalls or delays in external assistance—and to a lesser extent by domestic policy slippages.

While the 12-month rate of growth of broad money has decelerated markedly since 1985/86, it has displayed sizable fluctuations from year to year. In particular, in the aftermath of the introduction of a flexible exchange rate system in early 1986, broad money growth accelerated from 25 percent in the year ended June 1986 to 44 percent by June 1987, before declining steadily to 8 percent by June 1989 (Chart 8 and Table 12). The external shocks that took place in the first half of 1989/90 induced a reacceleration of monetary expansion to 22 percent by December 1989, but the tightening of financial policies and the recovery in export receipts in the second half of the fiscal year contributed to bringing broad money growth back to 4 percent by March 1991. However, the shortfalls in external assistance (whose monetary impact was not completely offset by a lower improvement in the net foreign assets position of the banking system) and the fiscal slippages in late 1990/91 and the first half of 1991/92 led to a worrisome pickup in the growth in broad money to 25 percent by December 1991. The corrective fiscal measures implemented in response to this slippage were expected to facilitate large net repayments by the Government to the banking system, which would allow a significant contraction in the outstanding stock of broad money during the last quarter of 1991/92.

With the benefit of hindsight, it would appear that the excessive expansion in reserve money that took place in 1985/86, 1986/87, and more recently, during the first half 1989/90 and during the period from March to December 1991 was translated primarily into a buildup of excess bank cash reserves

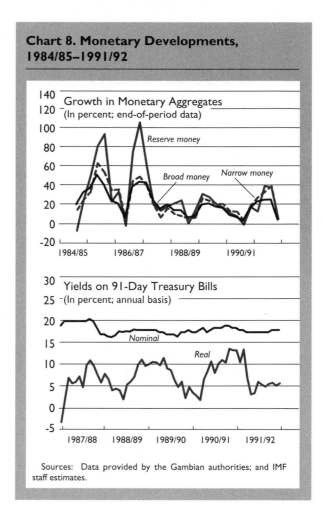

Chart 8. Monetary Developments, 1984/85–1991/92

Sources: Data provided by the Gambian authorities; and IMF staff estimates.

and in part in an acceleration in the rate of growth of broad money, and thus had a much smaller impact on exchange rate and price developments. The effects of fluctuations in the rate of growth of broad money on output growth appear also to have been modest in the short term, as output developments in The Gambia tend to be dominated by the effects of changes in the weather and other exogenous factors rather than by changes in domestic demand. The observed limited impact of the sharp variability in domestic liquidity conditions (i.e., reserve money and excess bank cash reserves) on the growth of broad money and, in turn, exchange rate and price developments could be attributed to a number of factors special to The Gambia.

First, the monetary slippages emanated almost entirely from difficulty in adhering to the targeted ceilings on net credit to the Government from the

Table 12. Monetary Survey

	1982/83	1983/84	1984/85	1985/86	1986/87	1987/88	1988/89	1989/90	1990/91	1991/92 Est.
					(In millions of dalasis; end of period)					
Net foreign assets	−179.7	−298.5	−282.5	−584.7	−313.2	−176.0	−149.8	−146.3	143.4	426.2
Monetary authorities	−179.7	−300.6	−300.8	−595.4	−333.4	−192.1	−155.8	−166.9	115.1	391.2
Foreign assets	(18.3)	(24.4)	(14.9)	(11.4)	(97.7)	(255.8)	(232.4)	(281.9)	(553.3)	(862.3)
Foreign liabilities	(−198.0)	(−325.0)	(−315.7)	(−606.8)	(−431.1)	(−447.9)	(−388.2)	(−448.8)	(−438.2)	(−471.2)
Commercial banks	—	2.1	18.3	10.7	20.2	16.1	5.9	20.6	28.3	35.0
Net domestic assets	312.8	358.9	373.1	594.2	294.4	224.9	191.6	112.0	−67.2	−375.7
Domestic credit	344.3	396.6	415.2	501.3	326.0	256.2	241.9	174.4	58.1	−273.3
Claims on the Government (net)	73.6	77.5	92.0	100.3	−64.9	−37.5	−115.2	−115.3	−279.4	−632.3
Claims on the rest of the economy	270.7	319.1	323.2	401.0	390.9	293.7	357.1	289.7	337.5	359.0
GPMB[1]	(101.4)	(111.3)	(93.0)	(132.8)	(156.0)	(56.0)	(75.1)	(28.1)	(37.7)	(9.0)
Other public enterprises	(—)	(−49.4)	(71.2)	(84.6)	(60.7)	(45.5)	(57.4)	(11.2)	(10.1)	(13.8)
Private sector	(169.3)	(158.4)	(159.0)	(183.6)	(174.2)	(192.3)	(224.5)	(250.5)	(289.8)	(336.2)
Other items (net)	−31.5	−37.7	−42.1	92.9	−31.6	−31.3	−50.3	−62.4	−125.3	−102.4
Revaluation account	—	96.5	125.6	237.4	392.8	392.2	433.5	590.3	564.4	624.7
SDR allocation	—	−19.5	−33.6	−19.5	−46.8	−46.8	−48.3	−56.5	−56.5	−63.5
Broad money	133.1	137.4	182.6	227.4	327.2	394.3	427.0	499.4	584.1	611.7
Money	(...)	(77.5)	(96.5)	(129.5)	(192.4)	(222.1)	(235.2)	(282.0)	(334.3)	(350.1)
Quasi-money	(...)	(59.9)	(86.1)	(97.9)	(134.8)	(172.2)	(191.8)	(217.5)	(249.8)	(261.6)
					(In units indicated)					
Memorandum items										
Nominal GDP (in millions of dalasis)	605.8	617.8	781.9	1,085.2	1,486.0	1,635.5	1,942.3	2,345.2	2,689.4	3,117.2
(percentage change)	15.5	2.0	26.5	38.8	36.9	10.1	18.8	20.7	14.7	15.9
Velocity (GDP/average broad money)	4.6	4.5	4.3	4.9	5.3	4.5	4.8	4.9	5.1	5.0
Percentage change from previous year:										
Net domestic assets	39.1	14.7	4.0	59.3	−50.5	−23.6	−14.8	−41.5	−160.0	−459.1
Claims on the Government (net)	47.5	5.3	18.7	9.0	−164.7	42.3	−207.5	−0.1	−142.3	−126.3
Claims on public enterprises	90.6	58.5	2.2	32.4	−0.3	−53.2	30.7	−70.4	21.6	−52.1
Claims on the private sector	12.6	−6.4	0.4	15.5	−5.1	10.4	16.8	11.6	15.7	16.0
Broad money	35.1	3.2	32.9	24.5	43.9	20.5	8.3	17.0	16.9	4.7
Contribution to the growth of broad money[2]										
Net foreign assets	−54.2	−89.3	11.6	−165.5	119.4	41.9	6.6	0.8	58.0	48.4
Net domestic assets	89.3	34.6	10.3	121.1	−131.8	−21.2	−8.4	−18.6	−35.9	−52.8

Sources: Data provided by the Gambian authorities; and IMF staff estimates.
[1] The Gambia Produce Marketing Board.
[2] Twelve-month change as a ratio of the beginning-of-period money stock.

banking system, or difficulty in attaining the gross official reserve targets. With the exception of occasional overruns of credit increases to the GPMB, the expansion of bank credit to the private sector and public enterprises has invariably been below target. Thus, to the extent that the slippages in the government financial performance were quickly corrected, the monetary overhang was pari passu absorbed.

Second, the weak development of financial markets in The Gambia and the associated high transaction costs, a feature that is common to many developing countries, seem to have limited the ability of economic agents to quickly dispose of any "undesired" buildup in money balances by purchasing more goods or foreign exchange.[20] As a consequence, the temporary monetary overhangs have been reflected in fluctuations in the share of currency outside banks in broad money and compensating changes in the income velocity of circulation.

Third, excess bank cash reserves could not quickly result in an increase in bank credit, as the expansion of credit to the private sector in The Gambia is largely demand determined, given the limited size of unmet credit demand from creditworthy customers. The existence of a large portfolio of nonperforming bank loans to the private sector may also have restrained the commercial banks from taking on new customers without adequate documentation and collateral. The bulk of bank credit to the private sector in The Gambia is related to tourism and trade financing, particularly for re-exports. Traders involved in the re-export trade tend to finance most of their imports from their own funds or with foreign suppliers' credits, prompted in part by the high cost structure of the domestic banking system, limiting their domestic borrowing to the financing of the domestic currency costs of their operations.

The latter feature of the credit market in The Gambia has tended to insulate the banking system from the impact of the normal leads and lags associated with the rather volatile re-export trade, thus restraining the fluctuations in domestic liquidity conditions. At the same time, however, the lower-than-otherwise demand for domestic credit and, indirectly, dalasi-denominated financial assets by the private sector has limited the development of the domestic money market. The latter has tended to be characterized by sizable excess liquid assets

held by banks, mainly in the form of government securities. Notwithstanding the increasing interest of the nonbank sector to invest in financial assets, the demand for treasury bills at the biweekly auction has been narrowly based, while interest rate bids have tended to move only modestly in relation to changes in the inflation rate and the relative tightness or laxity of domestic liquidity conditions. As a result, the interest rate on three-month treasury bills has moved in recent years within a very narrow range, of 17–20 percent, giving rise to pronounced fluctuations in real interest rates, even though the latter have remained generally at positive levels. The Central Bank has on occasion participated in the treasury bill auctions by placing bids for the purchase of a small portion of the total amounts of bills offered, so as to signal to the market, by influencing the average treasury bill interest rate, its preferences with regard to the level of interest rates in the money market. As indicated above, maintenance of appropriate margins above interest rates abroad has been considered necessary to support the exchange rate policy.

Overall, despite the lifting of interest rate controls in 1985 and the variability in domestic liquidity conditions, interest rates in The Gambia have remained rather rigid. In response to the new policy environment, the three commercial banks raised initially their lending rate structure and lowered somewhat their deposit rates, thus increasing their interest rate margins from less than 10 percent to around 12–14 percent throughout the period since 1986. The widening of interest rate margins reflected in part an attempt by the banks to offset the impact on their financial position of the difficulties faced by several public and private enterprises to service their financial obligations to the banking system, mainly to the largest commercial bank (which was owned by the Government). In addition, difficulties in liquidating collateral to bank loans and long delays in enforcing financial contracts have added a sizable risk premium to bank lending rates. Bank deposit and lending rates have tended to be even less volatile than treasury bill rates, notwithstanding the variations in the banks' liquidity position since 1985/86. For example, the maximum lending rate on bank loans to the trading sector declined gradually from 30 percent in June 1986 to 26.5 percent at present, while the interest rate on three-month bank deposits fell from 18 percent to 12.5 percent, respectively.

The relative rigidity in the interest rate structure is attributable to a number of factors: (1) the thin domestic money and credit markets, the limited availability of financial instruments for investment, and the absence of a domestic capital market; (2) the oligopolistic and noncompetitive nature of

---

[20]This view is supported by the fact that, while the share in broad money of currency outside banks has declined somewhat in recent years, it remains high, amounting to 33 percent in March 1992.

the banking system (two of the three banks in the banking system have in fact been making substantial profits, in excess of 200 percent of their capital base per year); and (3) the weak arrangements for bank supervision.[21] For similar reasons, interest rate variability has also been limited in some other African countries that have lifted their controls on interest rates in recent years.[22]

Monetary Policy, Exchange Rate Policy, and Inflation

The emphasis of interest rate and reserve management policies on broadly stabilizing the nominal effective exchange rate, in the context of the policy of preserving external competitiveness, has contributed to a reduction in inflation. Given the openness of the economy and the expanding regional trade for goods imported through The Gambia, the main channel for the transmission of the impact of changes in the stance of monetary policy to price developments has been the evolution of the exchange rate of the dalasi, particularly of the bilateral rate vis-à-vis the CFA franc.

The increasing importance of the re-export trade has strengthened the sensitivity of the domestic prices of consumer goods that are prominent in this trade—mainly foodstuffs, clothing, and footwear—to developments in the demand and prices of these goods in the subregion. These consumer goods are imported in large quantities into The Gambia and, for the most part, are sold wholesale in the capital city of Banjul to visiting traders from the subregion. The bulk of these goods is included in the consumer price index (CPI) of The Gambia;[23] the CPI is actually measured on the basis of prices prevailing in Banjul and in two adjacent urban areas. As a result, price developments in The Gambia are to a substantial and increasing extent determined by changes in the nominal demand for the re-export goods by consumers in the subregion and, accordingly, are less sensitive to changes in monetary conditions in The Gambia. As the prices for the re-export goods are denominated in terms of CFA francs, consumer prices in The Gambia have tended to be strongly influenced by changes in the dalasi/CFA franc exchange rate (Chart 9). This influence could more easily be discerned in periods, such as the first half of 1991/92, when the dalasi weakened markedly against the CFA franc, even though the nominal effective exchange rate remained broadly stable. The impact on consumer prices of these developments, as well as of occasional disturbances in the supply of certain key food items, has tended to be accommodated by changes in the velocity of circulation.

Notwithstanding the increasing influence of changes in the dalasi/CFA franc rate on price developments and the relatively low inflation prevailing in the neighboring CFA franc countries, a formal linking of the dalasi to the CFA franc so as to provide a nominal anchor for price movements and inflation expectations in The Gambia has not been considered a desirable option by the Government.[24] Bilateral trade between The Gambia and the CFA franc zone is minimal (in terms of domestically produced goods), while The Gambia's tourism market and the prices and demand for its traditional and nontraditional exports are determined primarily by developments in European and other industrial countries. Accordingly, exchange rate policy remains focused on preserving overall external competitiveness. With the emphasis of financial policies on lowering inflation to a low rate comparable to that for the main trading partner countries, this objective is consistent with minimal changes in the nominal effective exchange rate. Given the link between the CFA franc and the French franc, stability of the nominal effective exchange rate would be equivalent to a stable dalasi/CFA franc rate, insofar as cross rates among the currencies of the major industrial countries remain broadly unchanged.

Financial Sector Reform

The banking system of The Gambia at the start of the reform efforts consisted of the Central Bank of The Gambia and three commercial banks: the

---

[21]Recent developments in the economic literature suggest that under conditions of uncertainty and asymmetric information between borrowers and creditors, and as long as banks are less risk-averse than their customers, it would be optimal for banks to keep their lending rates relatively stable and below the levels that would equilibrate the supply and demand for credit, so as to avoid financing riskier projects, and thus maximize profits. For details, see Stiglitz and Weiss (1981) and Villanueva and Mirakhor (1990).

[22]For a review of the recent experience with interest rate liberalization in The Gambia, Ghana, Kenya, Malawi, and Nigeria, see Turtelboom (1991).

[23]The combined weight of these items in the CPI of The Gambia is believed to be fairly high. This is suggested by the fact that imported food and beverages account for 23.9 percent, and imported clothing, textiles, and footwear for another 14.9 percent of the CPI basket of goods.

---

[24]For a recent assessment of the CFA franc zone, see Boughton (1991). A comprehensive review of analytical issues with regard to exchange rate policy in developing countries is provided by Aghevli, Khan, and Montiel (1991).

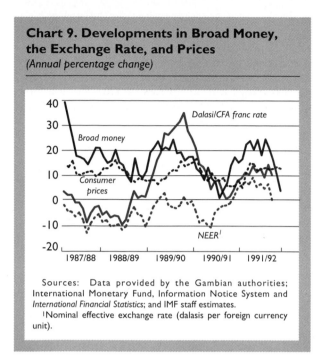

Chart 9. Developments in Broad Money, the Exchange Rate, and Prices
(Annual percentage change)

Sources: Data provided by the Gambian authorities; International Monetary Fund, Information Notice System and *International Financial Statistics*; and IMF staff estimates.

[1] Nominal effective exchange rate (dalasis per foreign currency unit).

Gambia Commercial and Development Bank (GCDB); the Standard Chartered Bank of The Gambia; and the International Bank for Commerce and Industry, which is a local branch of a Senegalese bank. A third foreign-owned bank, the Continent Bank, has recently been licensed. Other financial institutions included the Gambia National Insurance Corporation, the Government Savings Bank, and the Social Security and Housing Finance Corporation. An Agricultural Development Bank was created in 1981, but it soon encountered severe financial difficulties that led to a freezing of its activities in 1982 and to its eventual liquidation in 1989.

The centerpiece of the financial sector reform efforts since 1985/86 has been the rehabilitation of the GCDB. The GCDB had run into severe financial difficulties in the late 1970s and early 1980s, owing to a growing share of nonperforming loans and inadequate capitalization, and thus to growing recourse to refinancing from the Central Bank. A restructuring program was carried out between 1986/87 and 1988/89 with technical assistance from the World Bank, which provided for new capital injections by the Government, the consolidation of outstanding debt to the Central Bank, and the replacement with government securities of the nonperforming loans to public enterprises and to the private sector that had been guaranteed by the Government. The nonperforming loans were passed on to a new government agency, the Man-

aged Fund, which has been responsible for their recovery.

The management of the GCDB was reinforced in 1990 and, following an audit of accounts, its share capital was increased again in July 1990 and the bank was converted into a public limited liability company in preparation for its privatization. The GCDB was finally offered for sale in July 1991, and an agreement was reached in early 1992 with a recently established local affiliate of a foreign bank (Meridien Bank) for the purchase of a large share of the GCDB's assets and liabilities. The effective privatization of the GCDB was concluded at the end of June 1992, when the remaining nonperforming assets, net of certain liquid assets of the GCDB and of its liabilities to the Central Bank, were replaced with government financial instruments. The nonperforming assets of the GCDB, together with the remaining nonperforming loans in the hands of the Managed Fund, have been transferred to a newly set up government entity, the Asset Management and Recovery Company. The latter has received a strong mandate from the Government to recover as many of these debts as possible.

With a view to updating the legislative framework and bringing it more in line with the monetary policy reforms introduced in recent years, the Central Bank Act and the Financial Institutions Act were revised during the past two years, with technical assistance from the Fund. The revised Acts, which are scheduled to be presented to Parliament during the second half of 1992, allow for the introduction of central bank financial instruments so as to enhance the effectiveness of liquidity management and strengthen the provisions for bank supervision. Amendments to the Bankruptcy Act and the Sheriff Act are also currently being considered, so as to strengthen the procedures for the enforcement of financial contracts and facilitate the liquidation of collateral to bank loans. The bank supervision capacity of the Central Bank has also been strengthened with technical assistance from donors. The privatization of the GCDB and the revised financial legislation are expected to stimulate competition in the banking system of The Gambia and help narrow the existing large margins between bank deposit and lending rates.

The sequencing of monetary policy and financial sector reforms in The Gambia has been dictated by the adjustment needs of the economy and the lengthy process of preparing certain reforms, like the restructuring of the GCDB. The lifting of interest rate controls ahead of a strengthening of competition in the banking system and of the arrangements for bank supervision was necessary to support the establishment of a flexible exchange rate system and the liberalization of exchange controls on current and capital international transactions. While desirable, the restructuring and privatization of the GCDB could not be completed earlier, given the complexity of the initial financial difficulties and the need to identify and adequately document the existing nonperforming loans; shortages of skilled staff and the limited interest shown by foreign financial institutions to invest in the banking system of The Gambia have complicated this task. Similarly, an enhancement of the arrangements for bank supervision and of the bank capital requirements could not be achieved without a time-consuming revision of the existing financial legislation.[25] Appropriately, the abolition of credit ceilings and the shift to an indirect system of monetary control were effected only after the Central Bank had acquired adequate experience in open market operations. The effectiveness of this system of monetary control and the development of the domestic money market would be strengthened further by the envisaged introduction of new financial instruments by the Central Bank.

---

[25]For the optimal sequencing of financial sector reforms, see Villanueva and Mirakhor (1990), Leite and Sandararajan (1990), and Wong (1991).

VII   Public Enterprise Reform

At the beginning of the adjustment process, the public enterprise sector in The Gambia was largely inefficient, characterized by overstaffing and major financial and managerial weaknesses. This had given rise to pressures on government finances and to difficulties in servicing on schedule domestic and foreign loans undertaken by these enterprises. The public enterprise sector had expanded markedly during the period prior to 1985/86, to comprise 6 financial enterprises and 28 nonfinancial enterprises, of which 19 were fully owned by the Government.[26]

One of the key components of the structural policies implemented by the Gambian authorities since 1985/86 has been the reform of the public enterprise sector, with support from the World Bank. The broad objectives of the reform program have been to reduce the involvement of the public sector in activities that could more effectively be carried out by the private sector, and to improve the effectiveness and financial performance of the public enterprises that would remain for the time being in the public sector. The reform of the public enterprise sector was expected to (1) allow the Government to focus attention on key strategic enterprises that were considered crucial for the success of the overall adjustment efforts (e.g., the GPMB, the GCDB, and the Gambia Utilities Corporation (GUC)); (2) minimize pressures on the Government to provide new loans and equity to public enterprises; (3) free government managerial and financial resources and redirect them to priority areas identified under the adjustment program; (4) help generate cash proceeds for the budget through the sale of public enterprises; and (5) create an enabling environment for new private investment, management, and technology in the private enterprise sector of The Gambia, thus enhancing efficiency, promoting greater competition, and instilling market discipline. Overall, the public enterprise reforms, together with the improvement in the macroeconomic environment, were expected to stimulate private sector activity and help achieve the output and employment objectives of the Economic Recovery Program.

The public enterprise reform program has entailed an ambitious divestiture program and a broad range of policy and institutional reforms to improve the managerial autonomy and accountability of the enterprises remaining in the Government's portfolio. The Government has also committed itself to avoiding the creation of any new, or investing further in any existing, commercial public enterprises. The overall coordination of these efforts and the supervision and monitoring of the operations of public enterprises has been assigned to the National Investment Board.

Under the divestiture program, 20 enterprises were divested during the period from 1985/86 to early 1992 through a range of modes of divestiture. In particular, 13 were sold outright or were offered for sale, 4 were leased to the private sector, and 3 were liquidated; in addition, a government department, the Civil Aviation Department, has been transformed into an autonomous entity. As a result, the number of financial public enterprises was reduced from 6 to 3, while the number of nonfinancial enterprises was reduced from 28 to 11; the number of fully owned enterprises has in fact been brought down from 19 to 6. As the enterprises offered for sale have not as yet all been sold, the cumulative budgetary proceeds from the privatization program since 1985/86 have amounted to D 36.5 million, equivalent to about 1.2 percent of the GDP in 1991/92.

For the enterprises remaining in the Government's portfolio, several measures have been taken to improve financial performance, including (1) the liberalization of pricing and procurement policies, facilitating significant upward adjustments in utility tariffs to help cover underlying operating costs; (2) a strengthening of the management of several key enterprises, such as the GPMB, the GUC, and the GCDB, including through external technical assistance; (3) the restructuring of the enterprises' financial liabilities through the takeover by the

---

[26]Data on the financial position of the public enterprise sector as a whole are not available.

Government of nonperforming liabilities to domestic commercial banks and foreign creditors, as well as the repayment by the Government of sizable liabilities of certain major enterprises to the Central Bank; (4) the adoption by the Government of a firm policy not to subsidize the operating costs of public enterprises; (5) support of the rehabilitation and investment programs of a few key enterprises, like the GUC and the GPMB, by external assistance; and (6) retrenchment of surplus staff in some enterprises.

These measures were complemented with the signing of three-year performance contracts with all but one of the remaining fully government-owned enterprises, incorporating specific monitorable financial and other targets. The monitoring and assessment of the performance under these contracts has been entrusted to the National Investment Board. The system of performance contracts, combined with the other reform measures, has contributed to a marked strengthening in the financial position of several public enterprises.

While the implementation of the public enterprise reform program has been very successful and the results achieved are encouraging, several problems remain, most notably in the provision of electricity and other utility services by the GUC, which will continue to be addressed in the period ahead. In particular, it is envisaged that the management of the GUC will be leased to private operators and that the GPMB will be offered for sale during the second half of 1992.

VIII Social Impact of Adjustment

The Gambia's adjustment efforts since 1985/86 have contributed to a steady growth in real GDP and the stabilization, on average, in real per capita incomes, despite the stagnation in agricultural output. The increased availability of foreign exchange has facilitated greater imports of basic consumer and intermediate goods. The strong growth in activity in the industrial and services sectors stimulated the expansion of employment opportunities in the urban and formal sectors of the economy.

The benefits from economic growth have not, however, been evenly distributed to all segments of the society. The leveling off of agricultural output in the face of a rapidly expanding population, coupled with the marked decline in real groundnut producer prices, has resulted in a significant deterioration in the living standards of the rural population. These adverse effects reflected entirely the impact of unfavorable weather and the collapse of groundnut prices in world markets, and could not be attributed to the reform measures implemented by the authorities.[27] At the same time, the increasing urban migration has strained the provision of basic utility services (such as water and electricity supply) in the capital city of Banjul, as well as in other major urban areas, and has given rise to a shortage of affordable housing. While the living standards of traders and those employed in the urban areas have improved, the living conditions of the urban unemployed and underemployed has most likely worsened.

In the context of the overall economic strategy, fiscal policy has played a key role in alleviating the impact of adjustment on the most vulnerable groups in the short term and reducing poverty over the longer term.[28] The adjustment efforts pursued by the Government have focused on stimulating private sector activity and maximizing employment opportunities in both the rural and urban areas, as well as on improving the provision of basic education and health services and rehabilitating the economic and social infrastructure. Moreover, greater emphasis has been placed on the provision of agricultural extension and research services, and on improving the marketing arrangements for agricultural produce. As indicated in Section V, the share of outlays on education and health in total current government spending has been raised sharply in recent years. With donor assistance, the provision of health services in rural areas has been improved. Seven regional health centers have been upgraded to improve and expand services in rural areas, and maternal and child health services, including family planning, have been expanded. National immunization campaigns against childhood diseases have contributed to raising the national immunization average from 55 percent in the mid-1980s to 70 percent at present. A drug revolving fund was also established in 1988/89, with a view to generating sufficient resources for maintaining essential drugs and medical supplies at adequate levels.

To aid the retrenched civil servants, a special compensation package was provided to employees who had at least five years service, consisting of 1.2 months of salary for each year of service, over and above the normal pension benefits. In addition, a civil service resettlement program was established to provide (1) employment counseling; (2) access to basic entrepreneurial training and more specialized technical training, if appropriate; and

---

[27]The income position of groundnut farmers may have been alleviated in part by the sales of groundnuts across the border, where groundnut producer prices have in general been higher than those prevailing in The Gambia; the consumption of groundnuts by households in the rural areas may have also alleviated the impact of declining incomes on their nutritional intake, given the high calorie and protein content of groundnuts. The adjustment costs borne by individual farmers may have also been alleviated by the informal social security system that exists in many villages of The Gambia (complementing the traditional extended family system), whereby available staple food items are redistributed among participants through the local mosques; for more details on the informal social security system, see von Braun (1991).

[28]For the role of fiscal policy in improving income distribution under Fund-supported programs, see International Monetary Fund (1986).

(3) credit for the establishment of small business ventures in priority areas, such as agriculture, fishing, small-scale manufacturing, and tourism-related crafts.

Although the overall results of the adjustment efforts since 1985/86 have been positive, the Government has been aware of the hardships faced by the poorest segments of the population and has been monitoring closely the social impact of the reform program. In this context, women have been clearly identified as a particularly vulnerable group because of their relative economic and social status and the lag with which benefits reach them. A Women in Development project, financed by the World Bank and currently being implemented, is designed to (1) improve women's productivity and income earning potential; (2) strengthen government institutions to enable them to deal effectively with women's issues; and (3) contribute to bringing a change in the Gambian society's perception of the role of women. With donor assistance, a Social Dimensions of Adjustment Project is also being implemented, with a view to establishing a data base and developing analytical capabilities for the preparation of action programs aimed at improving the living standards of the poorest. In addition, high priority is being attached to reducing The Gambia's high rate of population growth, which is perceived as undermining the country's development objectives. To this end, a comprehensive national population policy is close to being completed, which emphasizes, in addition to the need to improve and expand the family planning and health services, a broad range of population-related issues, such as education, the environment, internal and international migration, and employment.

IX Concluding Remarks

The Gambia has made considerable progress since the mid-1980s in laying the foundation for a sustainable expansion of output through the successful implementation of a wide range of financial and structural reforms, supported by successive arrangements from the Fund and structural adjustment credits from the World Bank. As a result, by the end of the three-year ESAF arrangement, The Gambia's internal and external imbalances had been reduced and a comfortable external position had been attained, consistent with no need for exceptional balance of payments financing, mainly as a result of the significant progress made in diversifying the production and export bases.

This impressive performance can be attributed to four main factors: first, the strong commitment by the Gambian authorities to the adjustment process, as evidenced by their willingness to take prompt and appropriate corrective measures in the face of changing external circumstances and domestic policy slippages; second, the reliance on a market-oriented approach, entailing the early restoration of an appropriate structure of relative prices and the strengthening of economic incentives, notably through the shift to a market-determined exchange rate, the liberalization of the exchange and trade system, the lifting of all price controls, and the restoration of positive real interest rates; third, the pursuit of restrictive fiscal and monetary policies and the implementation of a broad range of structural reforms, including the scaling down of the size of the public sector through a far-reaching privatization program; and finally, the provision of substantial technical and concessional financial assistance from the international donor community.

The sequencing of the policy reforms has been appropriate and critical for the positive results that have been achieved. The removal of the distortions in the relative price and overall incentive structure, and most notably the establishment of a market-determined exchange rate, at the outset of the adjustment efforts has fostered the diversification of the economy. It has also allowed The Gambia not only to cushion the adverse effects of sharp declines in both the volume and price of its principal export commodity, groundnuts, but also to improve markedly its external position and normalize relations with its foreign creditors. In addition, the implementation of a broad range of adjustment measures in virtually all policy areas has sustained a sizable inflow of external financial assistance—notwithstanding the delays experienced in implementing some structural reforms—as well as improved The Gambia's macroeconomic situation and maintained real per capita incomes against formidable odds and despite the stagnation of agricultural output.

The Gambian economy, nonetheless, remains vulnerable to adverse external developments and changes in the weather, while it continues to be heavily dependent on external assistance. As the experience in recent years has demonstrated, the macroeconomic situation remains fragile, sensitive to regional developments, which have a pronounced effect on the re-export trade, and to delays or shortfalls in annual aid disbursements, which tend to exacerbate the effects of any financial policy slippages. The reforms already implemented and those under preparation appear also to have strained the public sector's management and implementation capacity, particularly at the sectoral level where significant delays or slippages from the envisaged policy path have been recorded. This experience clearly underscores the importance for the Gambian authorities of strengthening budgetary discipline and policy implementation, as well as of enhancing the monitoring of economic developments.

In addition, it is recognized that the base of output growth remains somewhat fragile, despite the commendable progress already made in diversifying production and exports. As the experience during the past few years has demonstrated, the attainment of a satisfactory growth in real per capita income depends critically on the existence of favorable weather, while the re-export trade, which provides a large share of tax receipts and accounts for an increasing share of output, is strongly influenced by regional political developments and changes in the tariff structures of neighboring countries.

It is clear that much remains to be done to consolidate the gains already made and address more forcefully the deep-rooted developmental constraints that confront the Gambian economy. The high rate of population growth, an underdeveloped human capital base, the paucity of natural resources, and the degradation of the environment continue to impede additional gains in real per capita income. While the development process will unavoidably be a protracted one, an important head start to this end has already been made.

References

Aghevli, Bijan B., and others, *The Role of National Saving in the World Economy: Recent Trends and Prospects*, IMF Occasional Paper, No. 67 (Washington: International Monetary Fund, March 1990).

———, Mohsin S. Khan, and Peter J. Montiel, *Exchange Rate Policy in Developing Countries: Some Analytical Issues*, IMF Occasional Paper, No. 78 (Washington: International Monetary Fund, March 1991).

Boughton, James M., "The CFA Franc Zone: Currency Union and Monetary Standard," IMF Working Paper, No. WP91/133 (Washington: International Monetary Fund, December 1991).

de Merode, Louis, "Civil Service Pay and Employment Reform in Africa: Selected Implementation Experiences," Division Study Paper, No. 2, Institutional Development and Management Division, Africa Technical Department (Washington: World Bank, June 1991).

International Monetary Fund, *Interest Rate Policies in Developing Countries*, IMF Occasional Paper, No. 22 (Washington: International Monetary Fund, October 1983).

———, *Fund-Supported Programs, Fiscal Policy, and Income Distribution*, IMF Occasional Paper, No. 46 (Washington: International Monetary Fund, September 1986).

———, *World Economic Outlook, May, 1992*, World Economic and Financial Surveys (Washington: International Monetary Fund, 1992).

Kapur, Ishan, and others, *Ghana: Adjustment and Growth, 1983–91*, IMF Occasional Paper, No. 86 (Washington: International Monetary Fund, September 1991).

Leite, Sérgio Pereira, and V. Sundararajan, "Issues in Interest Rate Management and Liberalization," *Staff Papers*, International Monetary Fund (Washington), Vol. 37 (December 1990), pp. 735–52.

Quirk, Peter J., and others, *Floating Exchange Rates in Developing Countries: Experience with Auction and Interbank Markets*, IMF Occasional Paper, No. 53 (Washington: International Monetary Fund, May 1987).

Sallah, Tijan M., "Economics and Politics in The Gambia," *The Journal of Modern African Studies*, Vol. 28(4) (1990), pp. 621–48.

Stiglitz, Joseph, and Andrew Weiss, "Credit Rationing in Markets with Imperfect Information," *American Economic Review*, Vol. 71, No. 3 (June 1981), pp. 393–410.

Turtelboom, Bart, "Interest Rate Liberalization: Some Lessons from Africa," IMF Working Paper, No. WP91/121 (Washington: International Monetary Fund, December 1991).

Villanueva, Delano, and Abbas Mirakhor, "Strategies for Financial Reforms," *Staff Papers*, International Monetary Fund (Washington), Vol. 37 (September 1990), pp. 509–36.

von Braun, Joachim, "Social Policy in Sub-Saharan Africa: Reflections on Policy Challenges," in *Social Security in Developing Countries*, éd. by Ehtisham Ahmad and others (Oxford: Clarendon Press, 1991), pp. 395–413.

Walsh, Brendan, "Interest Rates, Financial Markets, and Economic Development in The Gambia" (unpublished; Ministry of Finance and Economic Affairs, The Gambia, January 1991).

Wong, Chorng-Huey, "Market-Based Systems of Monetary Control in Developing Countries: Operating Procedures and Related Issues," IMF Working Paper, No. WP91/40 (Washington: International Monetary Fund, 1991).

Recent Occasional Papers of the International Monetary Fund

100. The Gambia: Economic Adjustment in a Small Open Economy, by Michael T. Hadjimichael, Thomas Rumbaugh, and Eric Verreydt. 1992.

99. Mexico: The Strategy to Achieve Sustained Economic Growth, edited by Claudio Loser and Eliot Kalter. 1992.

98. Albania: From Isolation Toward Reform, by Mario I. Blejer, Mauro Mecagni, Ratna Sahay, Richard Hides, Barry Johnston, Piroska Nagy, and Roy Pepper. 1992.

97. Rules and Discretion in International Economic Policy, by Manuel Guitián. 1992.

96. Policy Issues in the Evolving International Monetary System, by Morris Goldstein, Peter Isard, Paul R. Masson, and Mark P. Taylor. 1992.

95. The Fiscal Dimensions of Adjustment in Low-Income Countries, by Karim Nashashibi, Sanjeev Gupta, Claire Liuksila, Henri Lorie, and Walter Mahler. 1992.

94. Tax Harmonization in the European Community: Policy Issues and Analysis, edited by George Kopits. 1992.

93. Regional Trade Arrangements, by Augusto de la Torre and Margaret R. Kelly. 1992.

92. Stabilization and Structural Reform in the Czech and Slovak Federal Republic: First Stage, by Bijan B. Aghevli, Eduardo Borensztein, and Tessa van der Willigen. 1992.

91. Economic Policies for a New South Africa, edited by Desmond Lachman and Kenneth Bercuson with a staff team comprising Daudi Ballali, Robert Corker, Charalambos Christofides, and James Wein. 1992.

90. The Internationalization of Currencies: An Appraisal of the Japanese Yen, by George S. Tavlas and Yuzuru Ozeki. 1992.

89. The Romanian Economic Reform Program, by Dimitri G. Demekas and Mohsin S. Khan. 1991.

88. Value-Added Tax: Administrative and Policy Issues, edited by Alan A. Tait. 1991.

87. Financial Assistance from Arab Countries and Arab Regional Institutions, by Pierre van den Boogaerde. 1991.

86. Ghana: Adjustment and Growth, 1983–91, by Ishan Kapur, Michael T. Hadjimichael, Paul Hilbers, Jerald Schiff, and Philippe Szymczak. 1991.

85. Thailand: Adjusting to Success—Current Policy Issues, by David Robinson, Yangho Byeon, and Ranjit Teja with Wanda Tseng. 1991.

84. Financial Liberalization, Money Demand, and Monetary Policy in Asian Countries, by Wanda Tseng and Robert Corker. 1991.

83. Economic Reform in Hungary Since 1968, by Anthony R. Boote and Janos Somogyi. 1991.

82. Characteristics of a Successful Exchange Rate System, by Jacob A. Frenkel, Morris Goldstein, and Paul R. Masson. 1991.

81. Currency Convertibility and the Transformation of Centrally Planned Economies, by Joshua E. Greene and Peter Isard. 1991.

80. Domestic Public Debt of Externally Indebted Countries, by Pablo E. Guidotti and Manmohan S. Kumar. 1991.

79. The Mongolian People's Republic: Toward a Market Economy, by Elizabeth Milne, John Leimone, Franek Rozwadowski, and Padej Sukachevin. 1991.

78. Exchange Rate Policy in Developing Countries: Some Analytical Issues, by Bijan B. Aghevli, Mohsin S. Khan, and Peter J. Montiel. 1991.

77. Determinants and Systemic Consequences of International Capital Flows, by Morris Goldstein, Donald J. Mathieson, David Folkerts-Landau, Timothy Lane, J. Saúl Lizondo, and Liliana Rojas-Suárez. 1991.

76. China: Economic Reform and Macroeconomic Management, by Mario Blejer, David Burton, Steven Dunaway, and Gyorgy Szapary. 1991.

75. German Unification: Economic Issues, edited by Leslie Lipschitz and Donogh McDonald. 1990.

74. The Impact of the European Community's Internal Market on the EFTA, by Richard K. Abrams, Peter K. Cornelius, Per L. Hedfors, and Gunnar Tersman. 1990.

73. The European Monetary System: Developments and Perspectives, by Horst Ungerer, Jouko J. Hauvonen, Augusto Lopez-Claros, and Thomas Mayer. 1990.

72. The Czech and Slovak Federal Republic: An Economy in Transition, by Jim Prust and an IMF Staff Team. 1990.

71. MULTIMOD Mark II: A Revised and Extended Model, by Paul Masson, Steven Symansky, and Guy Meredith. 1990.

70. The Conduct of Monetary Policy in the Major Industrial Countries: Instruments and Operating Procedures, by Dallas S. Batten, Michael P. Blackwell, In-Su Kim, Simon E. Nocera, and Yuzuru Ozeki. 1990.

69. International Comparisons of Government Expenditure Revisited: The Developing Countries, 1975–86, by Peter S. Heller and Jack Diamond. 1990.

68. Debt Reduction and Economic Activity, by Michael P. Dooley, David Folkerts-Landau, Richard D. Haas, Steven A. Symansky, and Ralph W. Tryon. 1990.

67. The Role of National Saving in the World Economy: Recent Trends and Prospects, by Bijan B. Aghevli, James M. Boughton, Peter J. Montiel, Delano Villanueva, and Geoffrey Woglom. 1990.

66. The European Monetary System in the Context of the Integration of European Financial Markets, by David Folkerts-Landau and Donald J. Mathieson. 1989.

65. Managing Financial Risks in Indebted Developing Countries, by Donald J. Mathieson, David Folkerts-Landau, Timothy Lane, and Iqbal Zaidi. 1989.

64. The Federal Republic of Germany: Adjustment in a Surplus Country, by Leslie Lipschitz, Jeroen Kremers, Thomas Mayer, and Donogh McDonald. 1989.

63. Issues and Developments in International Trade Policy, by Margaret Kelly, Naheed Kirmani, Miranda Xafa, Clemens Boonekamp, and Peter Winglee. 1988.

62. The Common Agricultural Policy of the European Community: Principles and Consequences, by Julius Rosenblatt, Thomas Mayer, Kasper Bartholdy, Dimitrios Demekas, Sanjeev Gupta, and Leslie Lipschitz. 1988.

61. Policy Coordination in the European Monetary System. Part I: The European Monetary System: A Balance Between Rules and Discretion, by Manuel Guitián. Part II: Monetary Coordination Within the European Monetary System: Is There a Rule? by Massimo Russo and Giuseppe Tullio. 1988.

60. Policies for Developing Forward Foreign Exchange Markets, by Peter J. Quirk, Graham Hacche, Viktor Schoofs, and Lothar Weniger. 1988.

59. Measurement of Fiscal Impact: Methodological Issues, edited by Mario I. Blejer and Ke-Young Chu. 1988.

58. The Implications of Fund-Supported Adjustment Programs for Poverty: Experiences in Selected Countries, by Peter S. Heller, A. Lans Bovenberg, Thanos Catsambas, Ke-Young Chu, and Parthasarathi Shome. 1988.

57. The Search for Efficiency in the Adjustment Process: Spain in the 1980s, by Augusto Lopez-Claros. 1988.

56. Privatization and Public Enterprises, by Richard Hemming and Ali M. Mansoor. 1988.

55. Theoretical Aspects of the Design of Fund-Supported Adjustment Programs: A Study by the Research Department of the International Monetary Fund. 1987.

Note: For information on the title and availability of Occasional Papers not listed, please consult the IMF *Publications Catalog* or contact IMF Publication Services.